9/15

W9-CJE-278

OUT OF THE
ASHES

Help for People Who
Have Stopped Smoking

Peter & Peggy Holmes

Fairview
Press

Published by Fairview Press, 2450 Riverside Avenue, Minneapolis, MN 55454.

First Printing: September 1992
Second Printing: July 1995
Third Printing: April 1999

Printed in the United States of America
03 02   7 6 5 4

Cover: Laura Cogswell,
Cogswell Design Company, Mound, MN

ISBN 0-925190-57-8
Library of Congress Catalog Number 92-072161

Publisher's Note: Fairview Press publications, including *Out of the Ashes*, do not necessarily reflect the philosophy of Fairview Health Services.

For a free current catalog of Fairview Press titles, please call toll-free 1-800-544-8207. Or visit our website at www.Press.Fairview.org.

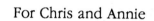
For Chris and Annie

Acknowledgments

We would like to thank the following people: Joe Zeitchick, for his original and brilliant work on addiction theory and treatment; Gillian Riley, for many brainstorming sessions over the years; Nathaniel Branden, whose work has had a profound and positive impact; and our editor, Lorrie Oswald for many valuable suggestions and much patience.

Introduction

The meditations in this book are the fruit of two experiences.

The first of these was our personal struggles with our own long–term addictions to nicotine. Each of us were heavy smokers for over 10 years. We tried many times to stop, but always returned to smoking eventually. We looked at various programs and kinds of help, but found all of them unsatisfactory for one reason or another—electric shock, behavior modification, self–hypnosis, smelling soggy cigarette butts, watching scary movies, these all seemed mechanistic, and inconsistent with human dignity. None of these methods gave us an intellectual framework for understanding addiction, or dealt with the questions we felt were important, such as, "Why is it that perfectly competent, functioning adults cannot just stop lighting cigarettes?" "Where does the loss of control in addiction come from, and, once lost, how is it regained?" Eventually, we developed our own method—a synthesis of objectivism (developed by the philosopher Ayn Rand), traditional 12 Step chemical dependency treatment principles, and the work of the Los Angeles addiction counselor Joseph Zeitchick.

The second experience, which enabled us to develop and refine these ideas, is the work we have done in our own program, Clean Break, to help thousands of people in the Twin Cities and New York stop smoking over the last ten years.

The need for a book like this is clear: Smoking is the deadliest, most underestimated form of drug addiction in the world. In fact, many experts consider nicotine to be even more addictive than heroin. But, while alcoholics and drug addicts have a variety of treatment modules available that include long–term, intensive aftercare, smokers do not. Most smoking cessation programs involve only a few hours of counseling or behavior modification, and then the smoker is left to his or her own devices. The abysmal success rates of these programs are stark evidence that many smokers need more than a short–term fix. Until most smokers have access to long–term treatment programs such as our own, this book can begin to fill that need.

Although this book can be used in conjunction with virtually any treatment mode, it reflects a particular view of addiction and recovery: The loss of control that addicts experience is psychological in nature, **not** physical. Although nicotine of course plays a part in tobacco addiction, the factors that determine whether someone can stop smoking are purely psychological.

Specifically, smokers cannot stop smoking because they have lost the ability to distinguish truth from fiction in this particular area of their lives. Recovery is largely a process of regaining that lost honesty. Second, smokers tend to make mistakes in logic when they think about stopping smoking that makes it very difficult for them to approach stopping responsibly. This is the source of much of the irritability and depression many smokers experience when trying to stop.

The first thirty meditations are intended to describe the basic ideas of our method in a logical, coherent order. Then various facets of the basic themes are explored and recapitulated. We suggest that you read the first thirty meditations through several times, and then explore—either at random, or using the index as a guide to those issues you find most relevant. None of these meditations will apply to everyone—nor are they intended to be read as gospel. They are simply the principles and ideas that we and many people have found most helpful and relevant.

This book is intended to be helpful, thought–provoking, and inspiring. It is full of practical, how–to advice that will help you stop smoking. The ideas and techniques it contains comprise a coherent and intellectually satisfying model of "how the world works," which is relevant and applicable to many other aspects of life. Lastly, we hope that the view of life this book contains—that life is a series of problems to be solved, and that real happiness is only attained by facing those problems bravely— will inspire you as you struggle with stopping smoking, and with life.

Cravings. . .

Smokers do not become non–smokers, they become ex–smokers. The distinction is crucial. Non–smokers are people who do not want to smoke. They have never smoked, and have no interest in it whatsoever. Ex–smokers, on the other hand, **do** want to smoke. It is just that they want to stop smoking even more.

I will never be a non–smoker. I will always have cravings, at least once in a while. But if I understand that these occasional feelings are the only alternative to smoking, I can treat them as a small price to pay for the freedom, better health, and peace of mind that I get from not smoking.

Cravings. . .

A desire to smoke is not a command which must be followed.

Just because I want to smoke—that doesn't mean I have to smoke. My craving is a feeling like any other. I can act on it, or choose not to. There is no such thing as an **overwhelming** desire to smoke.

Deprivation. . .

Imagine how you would feel if someone took away your cigarettes, locked you in a cell, and forced you to stop smoking against your will. Angry, anxious, depressed, outraged, scheming, defiant, self–pitying—these are a few of the responses that come to mind.

If you tell yourself, "I'm quitting. I can't smoke anymore," you are making a mistake in logic, a mistake which will lead to all the same terrible feelings you would get if you were locked up. "I can't smoke," really means, "I'm a prisoner. I have no choices. I am not free."

The truth is that I am always free to smoke. If I am not smoking, it's because I am choosing not to, not because I can't. Knowing this clearly defuses the sense of deprivation that I feel when I act like a prisoner.

Deprivation. . .

Smokers tell themselves, "I've got to stop smoking," all the time. This just is not true, and has a poisonous effect on stopping smoking.

No one has to stop smoking. It **is** a good idea. Sometimes it's even a matter of life and death. But no one has to do it. You always have a choice. Even people with advanced emphysema can smoke—and often do.

"I've got to stop," is untrue and irresponsible. It creates resistance and destroys motivation. "I'm choosing to stop," defuses that resistance, and enables me to feel free and strong about not smoking.

Moment by moment. . .

Life proceeds one moment at a time. There really is no such thing as "quitting" smoking. There is only dealing with the problem, one day at a time. All I can do is deal with my smoking here and now, and hope for the best.

I will decide tomorrow what I will do tomorrow. I will worry about the fishing trip next summer when the time comes. All I have control over right now, all I need to worry about right now, is this moment. And I can handle that.

One puff. . .

There are people who can smoke occasionally. The evidence of my life proves overwhelmingly that I am not one of them. Just like an alcoholic who takes one drink and goes out of control, taking one puff will almost certainly take me back to smoking. Maybe for a week, maybe for a year, maybe for the rest of my life. Knowing that it's unlikely to be just one puff, or just one cigarette, helps me think twice before lighting up.

Decisions. . .

I may want to smoke—but I want to stop smoking much more.

I can smoke—but I don't have to smoke.

I might smoke later, or I might not. All I need to worry about is this moment.

My options are to experience this craving now, or go back to smoking.

I choose, for now, to accept these mildly uncomfortable feelings, because they are the only alternative to smoking, and because they are the only thing in the world which will allow me to breathe better, live longer, like myself more, and be more alive.

Conflict. . .

Conflict is what you experience when you have two alternatives which are mutually exclusive, but you want them both. Examples would be spending your money and having it too, or smoking and stopping smoking. You think hard, do some soul searching, and make your decision. The next time you need to think a little less. Eventually you establish a pattern, and the decision (to not smoke, for example) becomes easy.

When you first stop smoking, it is useful and healthy to spend time in conflict. Thinking about what's more important. Agonizing. Soul searching. If you do this, each decision to not smoke becomes a little easier. And eventually it becomes easy and natural.

Decisions. . .

Being an ex–smoker means accepting desires to smoke. "Accepting" something is the opposite of trying to avoid it.

When I get the desire to smoke, I just relax my body and let the desire wash over me like a wave. Or I embrace it as the only alternative to smoking. I let it stay as long as it wants, and go on about my business while it's there. It was somewhat distracting at first, but with practice I learned to coexist with it peacefully. It's mildly uncomfortable, but it's not pain or suffering. It's just a fact of life.

Denial. . .

Just as there is no such thing as a happy drunk, there is probably no such thing as a happy smoker. Smoking is so inherently antilife, so contrary to a healthy person's values, that deep down all smokers must feel self–reproach.

I see evidence of this when my friends who smoke find out I'm not smoking. The excuses, the nervous jokes, the defensiveness all betray deep underlying unease.

Difficulty. . .

Almost everybody has problems when they stop, especially at first. Success does not mean **not** having problems or difficulty. Stopping smoking successfully means having problems and being able to work through them, sometimes quickly and sometimes gradually. These problems can include cravings, conflict, rationalizations, irritability, the desire to substitute food for smoking, and even relapses. If I understand that these feelings and issues are a normal part of stopping smoking, I can face and work through them in a positive way. If I expect stopping smoking to be effortless and smooth, I am much more likely to be thrown when I hit a bump.

Defeatism. . .

Hope is essential to recovery. For instance, in 12 Step Programs, the Second Step of recovery is, "Came to believe that a Power greater than ourselves could restore us to sanity." This does not have to mean a particular concept of God. It just means that for recovery to be possible, an addict must be open to the possibility of recovery, and that he or she will need help along the way.

When I start to think in hopeless or defeatist terms, I am not only endangering my abstinence—I am thinking unrealistically. There is nothing wrong with me. There is no reason I cannot successfully stop smoking. I can do it, and I am doing it.

Responsibility. . .

Avoiding situations where you usually smoke—sitting down with a cup of coffee, having a beer after work, socializing with friends who smoke—is to act out the principle: "In certain situations, I cannot be responsible for my actions. I cannot trust myself. I am at the mercy of forces outside myself." This belief is fundamentally irresponsible.

Today I will live my life just as I normally would. I will do anything I would do as a smoker. If I get a desire to smoke, I can choose to act on it, or not. There is no situation which can force me to smoke, or undermine my resolve if I don't let it. No matter where I am or what is going on around me, I am capable of not smoking.

Moment by moment. . .

Having a choice means you always have a choice. But, choice only lasts for the moment in which it is made. No matter what you say now, you can change your mind one second later. One of the big secrets of stopping smoking is doing it one moment at a time.

If I try to commit myself to never smoke again, I will feel trapped and deprived. My choice to not smoke is for here and now **only**. This enables me to feel free. And I can always handle not smoking for one moment.

Peter & Peggy Holmes

Avoidance. . .

Desires to smoke are inevitable. Part of being an ex–smoker is wanting to smoke at times. If you spend time with these feelings, they become easy to handle.

In the beginning, I needed to think long and hard about each desire. "What should I do?" "What's more important to me?" But with each desire I faced, and each decision I made, it became a little easier to not smoke. Desires to smoke are not threats to be avoided. They are opportunities to practice making decisions. And the more you practice, the easier not smoking gets.

Motivation. . .

All smokers have years, if not decades, of smoking experience—the shame, the guilt, the complete lack of control, the physical deterioration, the obsession to stop.

And yet when people quit, they often can not remember anything bad about smoking. As a matter of fact, smoking starts to seem far better than it ever did in real life—until they go back to smoking.

I want to remember what smoking was **really** like—not just the first cigarette, but the tenth, the hundredth, the thousandth.

Rationalization. . .

Thinking is processing information logically to arrive at the answer that is true. **Rationalization** is processing information illogically to arrive at the answer you want. The motive for rationalizing is always to avoid doing something you know you should do, or to justify doing something you know you should not.

As a smoker I spent years concocting elaborate lies to justify doing something I knew wasn't in my best interest. My abstinence depends on struggling to think honestly.

Cravings. . .

Many smokers are terrified that they will get cravings after they stop. They can not imagine being able to get that feeling without acting on it. And their view of the desire to smoke as an irresistible force creates a self–fulfilling prophecy.

Desires to smoke, like other impulses, are not irresistible. Just as you don't buy everything you want whether you can afford it or not, you don't have to smoke—even if you want to—if stopping smoking is more important to you. You may want to smoke sometimes, but there is no reason to be afraid of that feeling. It's just a feeling, and can never make you do anything.

I will not be afraid of cravings. I am perfectly free to **not** act on them.

Feelings. . .

Feeling is a mixed blessing; there is pain as well as joy in life. But if you are not willing to feel, you lose the good as well as the bad.

My commitment to stopping smoking is not just a desire for better breathing. It is a choice to be open to what is inside me and around me. It is a willingness to experience life without a cushion. The price is that the pain is more painful—but is worked through more quickly. The reward is that the happiness is more deeply satisfying—and lasts longer.

Difficulty. . .

There is no free lunch. Anything worth having requires effort. And this is especially true of stopping smoking.

To successfully control my addiction I need to accept moments of craving and make decisions to forego instant gratification for the greater long–term satisfaction. I need to spend time occasionally in conflict, thinking about what's important to me and what kind of life I want to have. I need to work at honesty and keep stopping smoking a high priority. If I don't bemoan the intrinsic difficulty of stopping smoking—I can welcome it as a worthwhile task, freely chosen.

Difficulty. . .

Like almost anything important, stopping smoking involves difficulty. A lot of difficulty for a few days, less and less as time goes on.

If I remember and expect this, I handle the difficulty well. It's when I want the whole problem to just be gone—when I want magic—that I get into trouble. I will try to remember that moments of difficulty are perfectly normal in stopping smoking, and take those moments in stride.

Responsibility. . .

Smoking is a decision people make—it is never the "fault" of external circumstances.

Although I often smoked in response to external "triggers," each cigarette I lit was a decision for which I am responsible. The trigger was never the cause of my smoking—it was just the moment I made the choice to smoke. The source of my actions was the decision I made.

There is no situation, stress, or craving which can make me smoke. I am capable of maintaining my abstinence no matter what is happening inside me or around me. Nothing can make me smoke except me.

Confidence. . .

Confidence is, "I have a problem and I can deal with it." False confidence is, "I don't have a problem anymore."

If I start to take my abstinence for granted, I stop watching for the traps my addiction still lays for me. I feel confident about my ability to deal with my smoking problem, but I must never forget I have that problem.

Awareness. . .

Smoking, like other addictions, has an anaesthetizing effect. It temporarily pushes away feelings. When smokers say, "Smoking helps me concentrate,"or, "Smoking helps me deal with stress," this is what they are talking about.

Seeking this escape really creates more problems than it solves. While lighting a cigarette may bring the illusion of short term relief, it really just ensures that the problem causing the unhappiness will not get dealt with.

My commitment to stopping smoking is also a commitment to be engaged with life.

Difficulty. . .

Smoking is passive.
Abstinence is active.

Smoking is stasis.
Abstinence is growth.

Smoking is numbness.
Abstinence is feeling.

Smoking is despair.
Abstinence is hope.

Today I will not take the easy way out that leads to despair. Today I will do the hard thing that leads to joy.

Feelings. . .

"Your feelings are directly created by your thoughts."—Dr. David Burns, *Feeling Good*

If I think, "Stopping smoking is a rewarding adventure," I will feel excited and happy.

If I think, "Stopping smoking is a restriction and a loss," I will feel miserable and depressed.

If I think, "Who am I kidding? I can't do this," I will feel pessimistic and doomed.

If I think, "So far so good. I can do this as long as I want," I will feel optimistic and confident.

Self–Esteem. . .

Nothing damages self–esteem like smoking does. Most smokers say it is the single thing in their lives they feel worst about.

Higher self–esteem improves every aspect of my life. With good self–esteem, I am more likely to be ambitious, to seek out and cultivate healthier relationships, to be more creative and successful in my work to treat others with more respect and benevolence, and to be more secure, confident, and happy.

Difficulty. . .

An addiction does not break itself. There is work you need to do, and the more aggressively you do it, the more quickly the difficulty will be overcome.

For me, in stopping smoking, this work includes: spending long hours in conflict, thinking hard about the pros and cons of stopping smoking, and deciding over and over what my priorities are; using cravings as opportunities to practice making decisions to not smoke; questioning the rationalizations and evasions I used to justify my smoking; and using close friends, families, and counselors for support and encouragement, as well as a forum to practice talking honestly about my addiction.

Hope. . .

A bad self–image is a self–fulfilling prophecy. To expect failure is to ensure failure. Part of stopping smoking is reformulating your self–image to incorporate the possibility of success.

Whenever I think, "I can't possibly do this," I will immediately challenge it. "Of course I can stop smoking. I'm a competent adult who has accomplished many other things in life. My moments of defeatism are distorted thinking, not objective reality."

Responsibility. . .

Recovering alcoholics say, "Stay out of slippery places." This idea makes some sense, but there is also value in the opposite view, "Live your life normally."

If I avoid situations where I normally smoke, I am really saying, "There are some circumstances in which I cannot be responsible for my actions." This assumption puts me at the mercy of external circumstances.

On the other hand, if I simply live my life as I always would, and put myself in the situations where I normally smoke, I am saying, "The power over my life is within me. I can trust myself under any circumstances." This latter approach is far more responsible and empowering.

Conflict. . .

Time spent in conflict is time well spent. Thinking, or even agonizing, about what my priorities are is the only way to really and finally resolve the conflict.

I want to smoke—and I want to stop smoking. My conflict about which is more important is the major difficulty in this process. Resolving this conflict is my primary goal. The more I think about my priorities, the more I will reaffirm that I want to stop smoking.

Cravings. . .

It is normal for ex–smokers to want to smoke sometimes.

I got myself hooked long ago. I can never go back and be a non–smoker. But I **can** be an ex–smoker. This means that at times I will have cravings. There will be moments of conflict. If I try to avoid these feelings I get frustrated and depressed. But If I accept them, and treat them as a natural part of being an ex–smoker, they are no more than a minor inconvenience. I will expect and accept any cravings I get.

Honesty. . .

People who can not stop smoking are people who can not think honestly about that particular aspect of their lives. It is not their fingers and lips and lungs that are out of control—it is their thinking.

As a smoker, I trained myself to lie and rationalize. I pretended I didn't feel bad about my smoking, and made ridiculous excuses to justify it. I lied to myself so much it became hard to remember what was the truth and what was the lie. Sorting that out—learning to be honest again—is the key to my abstinence.

Guilt. . .

Just as pain is a life preserving mechanism which warns us when our body is in danger, guilt lets us know when our actions are inconsistent with our values and self interest.

The guilt I felt about smoking was a healthy, sane reaction to a very self–destructive activity. The absence of that guilt now is a sure sign that I am making the right decision.

Motivation. . .

One of the real enemies of motivation is "victim" mentality. If you see yourself as a victim—forced to stop smoking by people and circumstances—you will feel no motivation to stop. In fact, you will feel resistant, and try to sabotage the whole process.

A victim—someone who "has to" stop smoking—can not think about the pros and cons of stopping smoking. They are too busy resisting this coercion, and feeling angry and trapped.

Responsibility is the key to motivation. "It's my life. It's my body. I can smoke or stop. Now what do I want to do?" This starting point makes motivation possible.

Deprivation. . .

When an ex–smoker gets in a situation where they used to smoke, they will often experience a feeling that "something's missing", or a vague sense of self–pity. This comes from acting and feeling as if they have no choice about stopping smoking. It is as if someone has taken their cigarettes away. They think, "I **can't** smoke anymore."

Even though I am not smoking, nothing has been taken away from me. I am making an intelligent choice, and I can change my mind if I would rather be smoking. Today I will remember that I am as free to smoke as I ever was. Nothing is missing. If I am not smoking, it's simply because I am choosing not to, one moment at a time. Knowing this cuts through the self–pity I feel when I start to act like a victim.

Cravings. . .

Smokers will sometimes describe the following experience: They stop smoking effortlessly, there are no cravings or conflict, what–so–ever. It is as if the addiction had simply been lifted. Then, after a month or two, they suddenly and unexpectedly find themselves smoking.

I believe the addiction was not lifted. It had just been driven underground. These people had unconsciously repressed their desires to smoke, and did fine as long as those feelings stayed buried. When the feelings came back, they smoked.

I take it as a good sign that I still have cravings. The addiction hasn't been lifted—I'm dealing with it one craving at a time.

Confidence. . .

Sometimes the addict inside me says, "What's the point? You know you're going to fail eventually. Why not just smoke now and get it over with?"

Nonsense! Forty million Americans have stopped smoking in the last thirty years. They can't all be smarter and stronger than I am. There is **no** reason in the world why I can't do this.

Pleasure. . .

Was smoking really pleasurable? Or did it just relieve the withdrawal from the last cigarette? Addicts really just trade short–term relief for long–term misery. The concept of pleasure is largely an illusion.

I used to say, "I smoked forty cigarettes a day but only enjoyed three." I get much more pleasure from not smoking than I ever did from smoking.

Fear. . .

Exaggerated fear of returning to smoking sometimes is caused by a mistaken belief that one's personal worth is on the line. There can be a sense that, "If I smoke, I'm a bad person," or, "If I smoke I'm a failure."

This is not true. Inappropriately identifying your basic worth as a person with your success in stopping smoking makes the stakes intolerably high. Today I will remember that I'm a good person whether I smoke or not.

One puff. . .

Smokers often tell themselves, "All I want is one." That is a lie. If they smoke one, they will just tell themselves, "All I want is one more." And then they are off and running.

I will never be satisfied. No matter how many I smoke, I will always want more. One cigarette is too many—ten thousand are not enough.

Fantasy. . .

An alcoholic fantasizes that the next drink will make everything all right. For a gambler, it's the next race, and for a smoker it's the next cigarette.

If smoking accomplished the positive gains a smoker fantasizes it will, it wouldn't be addiction. There are things in life that will bring comfort, stimulation, relaxation, and satisfaction, but they're not addictions. They are healthy relationships, interesting and challenging work, inner strength, discipline and self-directedness, maturity, self-acceptance, and self-esteem. One aspect of addiction is the endless search for a miraculous solution to life's obstacles.

I may want to smoke, but that doesn't mean smoking will help me; a cigarette is just a fix.

Humility. . .

There but for the grace of God go I.

I am not "cured." I am not better than people who are still smoking. I have no right to preach at them, judge them, or look down on them. Instead I should treat them with respect, wish them good luck, and keep my fingers crossed for my own continued success.

Here and now I am not smoking. Tomorrow I might be. That uncertainty is one of my strongest allies—it keeps me on my toes.

Rationalization. . .

Smokers lie to themselves. They do not look at themselves in the mirror and say, "I'm an addict fixing thirty times a day and slowly killing myself in the process." Instead, they say, "I enjoy smoking." "Smoking is a sign of intelligence and independence." "Smoking is one of those necessary vices that make life worth living." This dishonesty enables them to continue smoking without feeling too badly about it.

My smoking was not a bad habit. It was not a guilty pleasure. It did not help me cope. It was a drug addiction, pure and simple. An addiction that was really messing up my life. My motivation to remain abstinent depends in part on my being brutally honest about this point.

Motivation. . .

Although smoking has become increasingly unacceptable in social situations, the best motivations for stopping smoking are those that do not involve other people or their approval. Health, self esteem, quality of life, peace of mind—these are good examples of positive, personal motivation.

I am the only person who is always here. I am the person whose approval is most important. And the best motivations are those which I—not just other people—care about.

Empathy. . .

It is better to influence people by example than by preaching.

One of my friends who smokes has been watching my progress. She hasn't said anything, but it's clear she is very interested, and has a lot of mixed feelings about it.

I feel sorry about what she is going through. I know she feels bad about her smoking, but is afraid to try and stop.

The best thing I can do now is let her know that my feelings for her are unconditional. She is my friend whether she smokes or not. I hope my own example will give her the hope and courage to try and stop smoking, but I will give her room to make her own choices.

Being an addict. . .

Surprisingly, even in this day and age, many smokers have trouble with the idea that they are addicts. For many people, the label "addict" conjures up visions of winos passed out in the gutter.

I know now that perfectly decent, respectable people can be addicts. Addiction is not a sign of moral failure. It should be viewed as a disease some people are predisposed to, or a trap people fall into and then cannot escape without help. Acknowledging the truth is the beginning of recovery.

Substitutions. . .

Stopping smoking means working through difficulty. It involves feeling cravings, experiencing conflict, and being uncomfortable at times. If you embrace this difficulty, it diminishes quickly. But if you attempt to avoid it, the discomfort persists.

Eating more, drinking more, sleeping more, staying busy, avoiding situations where you'll want to smoke, all prolong this period of difficulty. These things seem to help in the short run, but the feelings you've covered up will just resurface later.

The easiest way to stop smoking is to live your life normally. Eat, drink, sleep, and act normally. Allow the cravings and conflict to arise normally. Experience the difficulty, and it will diminish quickly.

Guilt. . .

"The essence of guilt, whether major or minor, is moral self–reproach: I did wrong when it was possible for me to do otherwise. Guilt always carries the implication of choice and responsibility, whether we are consciously aware of it or not."— Nathaniel Branden, *Honoring The Self*

I do not have a choice about being an addict. So it is not appropriate to beat myself up. However, I absolutely have a choice about whether or not to act on that addiction. Therefore, it is appropriate to feel guilty if I smoke, and natural to feel good if I don't.

Moment by moment. . .

There is no such thing as quitting smoking. There is only stopping right now.

"I might smoke again." When I say this, my friends are sometimes concerned. But I'm convinced that this is a healthy and useful way to look at things. First, it's true.

Second, it's liberating. What a relief that I don't need to answer now for what I will do in the future. All I need to worry about is right now—and that's easy.

Benefits. . .

Sometimes the connection between action and reward is not readily apparent. Things we do today will have results later we cannot imagine now.

For example, I am often conscious of being more present, less distracted, in social situations. I'm sure this is an ancillary benefit of improved health, higher self–esteem, and the freedom I now have from the distractions of smoking. But when I first stopped I had no idea that what I was doing would pay off in this way.

Stopping smoking is such a profound act of growth, it's effects are so diffuse, subtle, and all–pervasive that there are bound to be benefits we do not foresee.

Rebellion. . .

Smoking is not freedom—it is slavery.

I used to say, "No one's going to tell me what to do. I'll smoke whether they like it or not." I thought of myself as a rebel because I smoked!

That seems pretty funny now. Cigarettes led me around by the nose. It didn't matter what I was doing—I would interrupt it if I wanted to smoke. I would find excuses to get away from situations where smoking was difficult—situations I would have enjoyed otherwise. I wasn't a rebel—I was a slave.

Relapse. . .

You never have your problem licked.

I have been surprised by several of my friends who returned to smoking after a year or more of abstinence. They seemed to be doing so well. After quite a few months of successfully staying off smoking, I now see more clearly the trap they may have fallen into.

It really has gotten much easier to stay off smoking. Some days I don't think of smoking at all. I have caught myself ignoring cravings because, "all that is behind me." But I know this is a very risky approach to take towards my addiction. If I take my recovery for granted, and if I don't put appropriate effort and energy into dealing with my problem, I am setting myself up for a fall.

Confidence. . .

Thinking about the future can be a source of fear, or a source of inspiration and excitement.

Because I have gone back to smoking many times in the past, I can sometimes slip into a feeling of hopelessness or pessimism about the future.

I can stop smoking. I am the author of my own life. I can create any scenario I want. I am not doomed to repeat mistakes I have made in the past. I always have the opportunity to change, improve, and grow. One moment at a time, I can create any future I want.

Difficulty. . .

Smoking is much harder than not smoking. You need to light and smoke the stupid things. You need to keep track of your supply so you don't, God forbid, run out. You need to clean up after yourself, and try to minimize the horrible odor smoking creates. You have a constant strain on your budget. You need to make and break resolutions to stop smoking, and rationalize how by the time you get cancer, someone will have found a cure.

I used to say, "It's just easier to go on smoking for now." Since I've stopped smoking I see that that's totally wrong. Stopping smoking is difficult initially, but very quickly it becomes a lot easier than smoking.

Happiness. . .

Stopping smoking is not a loss—it is a gain.

I have not given up anything, and nothing is being pushed on me. I am not trapped. I have no reason to feel sorry for myself, or be angry at anyone.

Instead I am freely choosing a new way of life. It involves minor difficulty at times, but also fantastic rewards I couldn't get in any other way.

As long as I take responsibility for the fact that I am stopping smoking of my own free will, I will experience it as a positive step, not a restriction or an injustice.

Responsibility. . .

When people stop smoking and become irritable, they are usually blaming the people around them for what they are going through.

This morning I was unusually irritable waiting to be served in a restaurant. I was feeling rushed and the person next to me was smoking—I wanted to smoke, too. By the time the waiter came I was furious. I blamed him for my feelings. In fact, it wasn't his fault that I was running late. He didn't make me want to smoke and he wasn't forcing me to deal with the difficulty of not smoking.

When I stop blaming others, and take responsibility for what I am doing, I immediately feel better.

Acceptance. . .

Part of dealing with problems is approaching them realistically.

If I want and expect no cravings or difficulty, I am guaranteeing that I will be frustrated and disappointed. On the other hand, if I know there will be moments where I crave cigarettes, and that I will need to think hard and experience conflict, I am much more likely to get through those moments. I am also much less likely to be alarmed and disappointed when those moments arise. Being honest and realistic about my problem is the first step toward dealing with it successfully.

Addiction. . .

One of the amazing things about addiction is that smokers are not more curious about their lack of control. Think about it, perfectly competent adults who swear over and over they will stop smoking, but go right on lighting cigarettes anyway. Imagine, if these people were suddenly unable to stop making left turns, or to hop up and down on one foot, how frightened they would be. They would search high and low for an explanation. But smokers accept their lack of control without question, and think it perfectly normal.

If I think about how strange and powerful a phenomenon addiction really is, I am much more likely to value my abstinence, and much less likely to take stopping smoking for granted.

Enslavement. . .

Above and beyond the wonderful health benefits of not smoking is a sense of satisfaction at being in control. Cigarettes led me around by the nose. I smoked in situations where I knew others would be upset. If I had only enough money for food or cigarettes, cigarettes **always** came first. I went out late at night to get cigarettes if I ran out. I smoked butts out of ashtrays. I even smoked through bouts of pneumonia. And, deep down I felt degraded by this behavior.

I enjoy the dignity I feel when I am in control of my own life.

Benefits. . .

Several studies have been published lately about how smoking creates tension. First, nicotine causes heart rate and blood pressure to go up. The level of adrenaline in the bloodstream increases. Breathing becomes shorter, shallower, and more frequent. Often the muscles of the neck, chest, and jaw become tensed.

I am always interested in studies like this, and enjoy comparing them with my own experience. I am definitely more relaxed since I stopped smoking, both physically and emotionally. I no longer get a sore jaw from clenching my teeth. Less tension means I can feel my feelings and respond to others more naturally.

I'm just more alive since I've stopped smoking.

Guilt. . .

Deep down, all smokers feel guilty about smoking.

For example, some of my friends who smoke seem distinctly uncomfortable with the fact that I have stopped. They make excuses and rationalizations for why they don't, and seem anxious for me to agree or approve. I have never suggested to them that they ought to stop, but their own guilt drives them to make needless excuses and apologies.

Honesty. . .

When someone's behavior is out of control, that's really a sign that underneath their thinking is out of control.

I think my own inability to stop smoking was really an inability to be honest. I rationalized and played games so much as a smoker that I eventually became unable to remember what was true and what was not. My success in stopping has been the result of a struggle to be honest.

Pleasure. . .

Ex–smokers will sometimes say or feel: "Gee, wouldn't it be great to have a cigarette now?"

But would it really be great? How would I feel after I smoked that cigarette? Would my life be better? Would I feel proud of myself? Or would I just want to smoke more?

I strongly believe the answer to my question is, "No, it wouldn't be really great to have a cigarette now." It would be momentary relief of that addictive craving, followed by guilt, regret, and a real possibility of returning to smoking.

Longevity. . .

Stopping smoking makes life longer and fuller in many ways.

If I stay off smoking my life will be much longer. First, mortality studies show I am likely to live up to eight years longer if I don't smoke.

Second, I will have more time for living each day because I will need less sleep, and have more energy for life. I will not waste time every day lighting and smoking cigarettes. I won't need to deal with the chronic, time–consuming obsession to stop smoking that plagued me as a smoker. I will be able to use the time I spent focused on smoking to do more with my life.

Sharing. . .

Sharing with others is a potent source of strength in my stopping smoking. It is also a way of being straight with people, and an opportunity for intimacy.

It's very important to know I'm not the only person who's gone through this struggle. One of the real values of going to Smoker's Anonymous, or sharing with a friend who has stopped smoking, is the sense of solidarity and acceptance that gives me. None of us is an island. We all need contact with and support from other people. None of us can do it alone.

Procrastination. . .

Thinking of stopping smoking in terms of a lifetime commitment is one of the main causes of procrastination.

I was the smoker who was going to stop tomorrow. I was constantly making resolutions to begin the next day, the next week, or the next month. And when the deadline came I'd put it off again.

This was a result of thinking about stopping smoking as a lifetime resolution, instead of as a moment to moment choice. It made "quitting" seem like a life sentence and I was never anxious to begin serving it.

If I keep myself firmly grounded in the moment, that desire to procrastinate disappears. Stopping smoking isn't an overwhelming life commitment—it's what I prefer for this moment.

Humility. . .

"Cunning, baffling, and powerful." This is how the addiction to alcohol is described in the book, *Alcoholics Anonymous*. It's equally true of smoking. Think about it—I smoked for years knowing it would kill me. I twisted my thinking into the most ridiculous distortions to justify smoking—and came to believe those distortions. I tried repeatedly to stop smoking and could not—and I'm not a stupid person.

Respecting your opponent is one of the first rules of strategy. What has enabled me to succeed this time is that I've developed a deep respect for the power of this addiction. I've stopped expecting an easy cure. I've become willing to work hard and struggle for recovery. I have made it my number one priority.

Tolerance. . .

Living in a diverse society means that compromise and mutual respect are necessary.

As a smoker, I tried to smoke courteously, but I took no abuse from non–smokers. As an ex–smoker, I assert my rights, but also respect the rights of smokers.

People have a right to smoke. It's their life. They will be the ones to pay the price, and as long as they aren't blowing smoke in my face, I will respect their prerogatives.

Cravings. . .

In the proper context, a craving can actually be a positive experience.

If I am experiencing a craving, it means first and foremost that I am not smoking. Secondly, it means I am getting the priceless benefits of being an ex–smoker. If the craving is the only alternative to smoking for the rest of my life, then having cravings sometimes is not such a bad deal.

Faith. . .

When all else fails, you proceed on faith.

On occasion I have a day where smoking and not smoking seem like equally bleak alternatives. I can't feel good not smoking and I know smoking would be horrible.

Sometimes I need to struggle through days like this without any guarantee that things will get better. 12 Step group members often call this "acting as if"—doing what you think is right and necessary, even if the payoff seems intangible or nonexistent.

Motivation. . .

Freedom is a prerequisite of motivation.

Knowing I ought to stop smoking is very different than wanting to stop smoking. In fact, the more I think of stopping smoking as an "ought" or obligation, the less enthused about it I am. Only when I free myself from the pressure of "oughts" and "shoulds" can I really want to stop smoking.

The more pressure I feel to do something, the less freely I can weigh the pros and cons of doing it. My mind shuts down and I resist. When I know I am free, however, I can ask questions, such as: "What are the costs and advantages of this course of action?" "What are my priorities?" "How do I feel about this?" Motivation and enthusiasm become possible.

Being an addict. . .

Experiencing conflict is a normal part of stopping smoking.

Sometimes I feel like I'm in an old Donald Duck cartoon. A little devil (with pitchfork) is standing on one shoulder, whispering in my ear: "Go ahead and smoke. You know you want to. No one will know. It won't really matter in the long run." On the other shoulder is a little angel saying, "Don't listen to him! He is the voice of temptation, while I am the voice of your conscience."

This is just the normal conflict that all addicts feel. The fact that I can view it in a detached, humorous mode means that I don't feel very threatened by my addiction, and can laugh at myself again.

Moment by moment. . .

Making assumptions about the future such as, "I won't be smoking anymore," is unrealistic and leads to feelings of imprisonment. Worrying about the future, "How am I going to handle the next craving," causes pointless anxiety.

I can't predict what I will do in any given situation yet to come. I can't know now whether I will ever smoke again. The most honest and comfortable approach is, "So far, so good." I can give myself credit for what I've done, stay out of the future, and keep on my toes—just for the moment.

Delusions. . .

Smokers lie to themselves to justify their smoking. Eventually they come to believe their own lies. These delusions make stopping smoking much harder.

For instance, if I believe deep down that smoking makes my life better or easier, I am going to want to do it that much more.

There is nothing good about smoking. It doesn't help me in my life. I feel better after a cigarette sometimes—but that's just because I'm temporarily out of withdrawal. I've squashed the craving—for a while.

Wanting to smoke is inevitable. Believing cigarettes help me is false and dangerous.

Deprivation. . .

"I can't smoke," is irresponsible, and leads to paralysis. This is one of the main reasons perfectly competent people can not stop smoking. This one treacherous mistake in logic makes it impossible to approach stopping smoking responsibly.

Control over the addiction comes from taking responsibility for my actions, "I can smoke. It's my life, it's my choice, it's my decision. Now what do I want to do?" If I start with the assumption that I have choices, there is a much better chance that I can make choices, and change.

Rationalization. . .

"Smoking was my only vice." The implication of this rationalization is that vices are good and somehow help you cope with life. Is this true?

Vices have come to be viewed as vices precisely because they hurt people—not help them. If I had cancer would I say, "Cancer is my only disease. Please don't cure me?"

Vices, like diseases, hurt people and hold them back. It is normal for an ex–smoker, like myself, to want cigarettes sometimes. But to tell myself that smoking (or any vice) is good is false and dangerous.

Avoidance. . .

Avoiding the situations where you normally smoke is just running away from the problem.

The only way I got comfortable in the situations where I used to smoke is by facing those situations. In the beginning I felt cravings, and experienced conflict about whether or not to smoke. But when I faced those feelings, and allowed myself to work through them, they diminished. Now the situations I most feared are usually easy to deal with. But I don't believe they would be easy now if I hadn't faced them and let them be difficult in the beginning.

Romanticizing cigarettes. .

It is one thing to say, "I want to smoke." It is something else entirely to say, "Smoking would be great." The latter represents a false value judgment that is a threat to long term abstinence.

One source of this distortion is an underlying feeling of deprivation. If I experience stopping smoking as imprisonment, rather than as a free choice, smoking will look much better to me than it really is. The forbidden fruit is always the sweetest. Alternatively, if I really try to emphasize that I am still free to smoke, but am simply making intelligent choices not to, I will be able to see smoking in more objective and unromantic terms.

Fear. . .

A little fear of—or a healthy respect for—this addiction can be a very useful thing.

Someone who gets behind the wheel of a car and drives without fear is a very dangerous person—to himself and others. A healthy fear is what causes drivers to be alert and cautious. Similarly, an ex–smoker who thinks, "I've got it made—I have nothing to worry about," is courting disaster.

I don't ever want to stop being afraid of smoking. Knowing that I will always be in some danger of relapse is what keeps me on my toes and dealing with my problem.

Irritability. . .

The way to defuse irritability is to accept responsibility for what you are doing.

On occasion I feel more irritable lately, and I know that it's related to not smoking. It's very important that I don't express this irritability, or dump it on the people around me. None of what I am going through is their fault. They didn't get me addicted to cigarettes. They are not forcing me to stop smoking.

The more I blame others, the more I will reinforce the image of myself as a victim being unjustly treated.

I have no reason to be angry at anyone. I am stopping smoking of my own free will, and if I don't want to deal with it, I can smoke.

Self–Denial. . .

Part of being an adult is accepting the fact that you do not get everything you want. The irony is that self–denial is ultimately much more satisfying than self-will run riot.

If I bought everything I wanted I would immediately be in severe financial trouble. I feel better managing my money responsibly. If I acted out every whim in my relations with the opposite sex, I would be in hot water pretty quickly. I'm much happier living within limits, and according to ethical principles. If I smoked every time I got the desire, I would pay a heavy price. Self–denial is much, much more rewarding in the long run.

I discovered long ago that it won't kill me if I don't get everything I want. Now, I'm discovering the same thing about smoking—it **won't** kill me **not** to smoke.

Awareness. . .

One facet of compulsive and addictive behaviors, like smoking, is that they mask feelings. And the more someone masks their feelings, the more they limit their ability to grow and achieve genuine happiness.

Some of the underlying issues here are: "Do I want to be present for my own life?" "Do I want to be aware or unconscious?" "Do I want to move forward, or stand still?" Smoking is not an isolated issue. It is intimately interlocked with the general direction and quality of my life.

Benefits. . .

Smoking damages self–respect.
I don't think there was a single aspect of my life I felt worse about than smoking. It lowered my self–respect, my general level of happiness, and hurt my performance in many areas of life.

Increased self–respect is one of the greatest benefits of stopping smoking. I am more ready to take on the challenges of life. I feel less afraid of people, and more at peace with myself. My behavior is in line with my values, and so I am more comfortable in my life.

Cravings. . .

Ex–smokers are **not** people who do not want to smoke anymore. They do want to smoke at times. It is just that they want to stop smoking even more.

It seems to me that this distinction is important. If I tell myself, "I don't want to smoke," then I will expect to have no cravings. On the other hand, if I am always careful to identify myself as an addict in remission, I will expect to have cravings and take them in stride.

Overconfidence. . .

It can be deeply satisfying to stop smoking—even exhilarating. But it is also important to keep your feet on the ground.

I have been dealing with this issue successfully for some time now. I am capable of dealing with it for as long as I choose to. But my smoking is a problem in remission, not a problem which has disappeared. I stop running scared at my peril.

Rationalization. . .

Smokers will sometimes rationalize: "What's the difference? I'm going to die anyway." Yes, but smokers die much sooner. According to the American Cancer Society, smokers who stop smoking before the age of fifty are twice as likely to live to age sixty five as those who continue to smoke.

It would be interesting to revisit smokers who use the, "I'm going to die anyway," rationalization on their deathbeds. Will they say, "I'm glad I smoked. I don't care if I could have had another ten years?" I doubt it.

I want to live as long and as well as possible. To pretend I don't care is to weaken my motivation to stay off smoking.

Tolerance. . .

When someone stops smoking, their smoking friends often react in strange ways.

Now that I'm not smoking, some of my former smoking buddies are uncomfortable around me. Some, who I consider good friends, have even "jokingly" tried to talk me into smoking. Although this behavior is shocking when you think about it, I know that it's really just a reflection of their own low self–esteem, and their guilt feelings about smoking.

I will refuse to play this game, and at the same time let my friends know that my stopping smoking is in no way a judgment about them. I will value them as friends, and leave them to make their own decisions about smoking.

Commitment. . .

"Commitment" has two meanings. The first is: being dedicated to achieving a goal. The second is being confined against your will. It is essential to make this distinction when stopping smoking.

I am committed to stopping smoking in the sense that I care deeply about it, and am willing to work hard to remain abstinent. I am not committed to stopping smoking in the sense that I don't have a choice about it, or that I have promised I will never smoke again.

When I use commitment in the first sense, I feel I am freely choosing to pursue a goal that is important to me. When I use commitment in the second sense I experience stopping smoking as a prison, a loss, or a burden.

Pleasure. . .

A lot of the changes which take place when you stop smoking are so subtle you do not really see them from day to day. But sometimes something reminds you.

A friend of mine is stopping smoking. She seems continuously preoccupied. She's jumpy, irritable, and I can see she's having a hard time.

When I watch her I see how far I've come, and how much of the work I have behind me. I empathize with her, and feel real pleasure in what I've accomplished so far.

Cravings. . .

Smokers and ex–smokers both get cravings. The smoker smokes to push the craving away temporarily. The ex–smoker accepts the minor discomfort of cravings to get the rewards of not smoking. One trades short–term relief for long–term misery. The other accepts short–term discomfort for long–term freedom. I'm glad that for now I'm making the latter choice.

Difficulty. . .

Many smokers have incredibly unrealistic expectations when they stop smoking. They expect to throw away their cigarettes, forget about them, and go on with their lives.

Smoking is an addiction—physical, mental, and spiritual. And stopping smoking entails struggle and growth in each of these areas. Physically there is the discomfort of withdrawal and cravings. Mentally, the task is to stop rationalizing and denying, and become more honest. Spiritually, stopping smoking is a chance to become more integrated, more at peace with yourself and your place in the world.

If I view stopping smoking as a rewarding struggle I can face and overcome the difficulty involved. If I expect magic, I will fail.

Happiness. . .

Acting has if you have no choice about stopping smoking dulls motivation and enthusiasm.

If someone locked me up, took away my cigarettes, and forced me to stop smoking, I would be utterly incapable of seeing anything good about not smoking. I would not feel grateful—I would want to escape and kill my tormentor. Similarly, if I think of stopping smoking as something I have no choice about, something I am obligated to do, it becomes gray, dull, unpleasant.

I do not have to stop. I am free to smoke if I choose to.

Knowing my abstinence is a free choice is the key to feeling good about it.

Honesty. . .

"Accepting what is" means living as an ex–smoker, with the moments of difficulty and the wonderful rewards that are both part of the package. "Wishing for what is not," means hoping for magic and being continually unhappy with reality.

I can accept what is, or I can wish for what is not. I got myself hooked on cigarettes long ago. I wish I hadn't, but I did. I will always have cravings at times. I wish this were not true, but it is. There is no magic that will make my problem go away. I wish there were, but there isn't.

Motivation. . .

A healthy fear of the consequences of smoking is an important part of the motivation to stop. But there is another necessary component which people often neglect.

By stopping smoking, I greatly diminish my chances of getting cancer, heart attacks, strokes, and emphysema. But I also create other benefits, in which I can take a genuine pleasure which goes far beyond the mere absence of fear. I can smell the air on a beautiful day in the country. I can feel more relaxed and clean. I have a freedom I haven't known in years. No matter what happens with my health or life in the future, these are consequences of stopping smoking I can take real pleasure in today.

Substitutions. . .

When people stop smoking, their other appetites often increase initially.

For instance, for the first week or so after I stopped smoking, I felt much hungrier than usual. I know now that my mind was trying to trick me. If I was stuffing my face, I wouldn't be feeling the difficulty of stopping smoking. Unfortunately, when the substitution stopped working, and the cravings for cigarettes came back, I would not have learned how to deal with them, and I would probably smoke.

Now, when I get a suspicious hunger, thirst, or energy I tell myself, "What I really want is to smoke." And I choose to experience the feeling as a part of the stopping smoking process, just as I would a desire to smoke.

Grieving. . .

It can be argued that going through a "mourning period" for cigarettes is the result of a mistaken value judgment—that cigarettes are a valuable and useful part of life. It is appropriate to mourn for the loss of something valuable—a loved one, or a valued possession. But would you mourn a cancerous tumor after the surgeon removed it? Would you grieve a ball and chain when they were removed?

I spent years justifying and making excuses for my smoking. "It helps me concentrate." "It helps me deal with stress." "It comforts me."

The more clear I get that cigarettes really weren't helping my life—quite the contrary—the less I mourn my cigarettes, and the happier I am that I'm not smoking.

Confidence. . .

The limitations we place on ourselves are what hold us back the most. "I can't stop smoking," "I'm bound to fail someday," "This is too much for me," all become self–fulfilling prophecies.

There is no reason in the world why I can't stop smoking. If I am willing to do what it takes, ask for the help I need, and let nothing get in my way, I can succeed at this.

Deprivation. . .

It is impossible to miss something that you **can** have.

When I start to miss smoking I'm misinterpreting my situation. I'm feeling as though I'm no longer free to smoke, like smoking has been taken away from me. In fact, I'm as free to smoke now as I've ever been. Even though I may want to smoke, nothing is missing. I'm not giving up smoking—I'm choosing something better. Knowing I can smoke changes that sense of loss into a sense of gain.

Cravings. . .

Stopping smoking involves paying a price to get a reward.

Every time I get a craving, I make a mental picture of four or five physical and psychological benefits of not smoking. And I tell myself, "This craving is my key to getting those benefits. If I want the rewards, I need to pay the price. The fact that I am having this craving now is a sign that I'm not smoking. That I'm choosing to be an ex–smoker, not a smoker. That I'm getting the fantastic benefits of not smoking. I can have cravings and rewards, or I can have smoking and its consequences. The cravings are part of the solution, not the problem."

Self–Image. . .

Nothing creates failure like the expectation of failure.

My repeated failures to stop smoking did damage to my self–esteem. I began to think there was something wrong with me, "I must be weak. I must have a death wish. I must be a loser." These negative self–images quickly became self–fulfilling prophecies.

I was astonished and thrilled, when I first stopped smoking, every time I got through a craving or crisis. Gradually it dawned on me that there was nothing wrong with me because I couldn't stop smoking, I just needed to keep trying.

This is one of the sweetest rewards of stopping smoking. I've become open to a much more positive, compassionate view of myself. Nothing creates success like the belief that success is possible.

Conflict. . .

Being in conflict involves long, often intense mental debates between yourself and your addiction. Your addiction will say, "Time to smoke!" Your rational self replies, "Wait a minute. I want to smoke but the cost is too high." "Smoking won't really hurt me. Stopping won't really help me."

It is extremely useful, especially when you first stop smoking, to deliberately spend time participating in this internal debate. Formulating replies to the enticing lies your addiction throws at you, trying to see through the falsehoods and get at the truth, even laughing at your addiction's creativity and deviousness—all will help you to overcome the addiction to smoking.

Guilt. . .

Guilt is a sign that our actions are not consistent with our values and self–interest. As such, guilt can be understood as a powerful and valuable stimulus to change.

Rationalizations are attempts to reduce guilt without changing the destructive behavior which gives rise to it. An employee who embezzles will tell himself, "Everyone does it," or, "My boss doesn't treat me fairly." A smoker will tell himself, "It seems as if **everything** causes cancer in rats," or, "What's the point of stopping? I'll probably get run over by a truck anyway."

If I allow myself to honestly experience my guilt about smoking, and see it as appropriate, I will have more motivation to stop.

Difficulty. . .

Smoking is much harder than not smoking.

As a smoker I was obsessed with stopping smoking. I thought about it all the time. Not a day went by when I didn't say to myself, "This is crazy. I've got to stop doing this to myself."

When I first stopped smoking, I was totally preoccupied with smoking for the first week or so. But the amount of time I focus on it has been declining steadily, and it is quickly becoming a very minor issue in my life. I think about smoking less and less all the time, and much less than when I was still smoking.

Gratitude. . .

Having integrity means that your actions conform to your values.

Apart and aside from the health risks and inconvenience, there was something about smoking that was "not okay" with me. I just didn't feel good about it on a fundamental level. It put me in conflict with my deepest values. Since I've stopped I feel more whole, more harmonious, more integrated.

Rationalization. . .

An addiction can cause your memory to play tricks on you.

Sometimes I think it would be so great to smoke again. But would it really? I have gone back to smoking many times. How did I feel after lighting up that first cigarette? Was I happy and proud? Did I pat myself on the back? Or did I feel regret and self–reproach? And what about after the second cigarette? The thousandth? Do I remember how I felt? Or do I need to go back to smoking to remember how painful it really is?

Realistic options. . .

Addicted smokers have limited options.

I can live with cravings sometimes, or I can go back to smoking. When I accept that those are the only two alternatives, cravings look pretty good. But when I hope for magic (like stopping with no difficulty or smoking with no consequences) the minor difficulty of cravings becomes hard to accept. If I accept the difficulty it's manageable. If I hope for no difficulty it's intolerable.

Dollars and sense. . .

Smoking is an expensive addiction. First, there is the cost of the cigarettes—up to $800 per year (and rising) for a pack–a–day smoker.

Then there is the time lost to smoking. Smokers pay more for insurance, and are sick much more often. The on–the–job absenteeism rate for smokers is double that of non–smokers.

And then there is the physical damage—burns and smoke stains in clothing, carpeting, and furniture. Some studies estimate the real cost of smoking a pack a day at over $2,000.00 a year (and rising.)

Imagine how I would feel if my boss walked in and gave me a $2,000.00 a year raise? That's what I'm doing for myself by stopping smoking.

Discouragement. . .

Studies show that for many people, stopping smoking is harder than breaking an addiction to heroin.

When I feel discouraged about the difficulty of stopping smoking, I am probably underestimating my addiction, and not giving myself credit for what I am doing. If I were dealing with a heroin addiction, I would expect to be hospitalized for treatment and to have follow–up care in a half–way house. I would also continue to go to 12 Step meetings frequently, for years. There just are not the same kinds of programs available for ex–smokers.

It's not that I'm doing badly. Stopping smoking is hard, and some difficulty is inevitable. When I look at my progress in that context, I can see that I'm really doing pretty well.

Humility. . .

None of us is perfect. Smokers deserve the same respect as anyone else.

I heard two people talking in a restaurant yesterday. One of them was vehemently putting smokers down, "Why should I have to breathe their smoke just because they're so weak that they can't live without a crutch?" He even said, "Smokers are pathetic!"

No one is perfect. We're all doing the best we can in a difficult world. Smokers have their weakness, overeaters have theirs, alcoholics have theirs.

It's OK to not want to breathe other people's smoke. But I don't want to start thinking I'm better than they are.

Difficulty. . .

No one said it would be easy.

Stopping smoking is hard some-times. If I remember that's how it's supposed to be, I can take that difficulty in stride, without regret or self–pity. It's when my expecta-tions are unrealistic, and I want everything to be easy, that I get into trouble.

No one said life is supposed to be easy. No one said stopping smok-ing is supposed to be easy. Fine. I'll willingly accept the occasional dif-ficulty to get the wonderful benefits of not smoking.

Honesty. . .

Changing mental habits is difficult, and takes consistent effort. Smokers practice dishonesty—they work hard to maintain the false justifications, rationalizations, and denials that allow them to go on smoking without feeling too terrible about it.

More than anything else, stopping smoking requires honesty. And changing those dishonest mental smoker's habits is the main work of stopping smoking. Repeatedly challenging the lies and evasions as they arise is the main psychological task of withdrawal and early abstinence. If practiced consistently, though, honesty (and abstinence) becomes easier and easier.

Awareness. . .

Sometimes the benefits of stopping smoking are not apparent until after you stop.

It was only after I stopped smoking that I discovered what a strong, obnoxious, and pervasive odor smokers emanate. My wife checked a book out of the library recently. After spending a few minutes with it, she remarked with distaste, "The last person who read this book was a smoker." The odor was that strong!

Even now, after months of not smoking, I will sometimes detect a faint odor of smoke on a suit I haven't worn since I smoked. I'm really glad I don't smell like that anymore.

Humility...

Pride cometh before a fall. Smokers who think they have their problem "licked" often get a rude surprise.

It would be false and foolish to think of myself as "cured." I have a life–threatening problem which, for this moment, is under control. But the minute I lose that healthy fear of smoking, the minute I become complacent, I am in serious trouble.

Motivation. . .

Smokers cover up their motivation by denying the consequences of smoking, and by creating fictitious "benefits" that smoking brings, such as, "It helps me unwind after work," or "It helps me to feel more confident in social situations." Uncovering motivation means looking at smoking more honestly. Smokers don't smoke because it helps them— they do it because they are addicts, and the price they pay is terrible. If this is squarely faced, motivation to stop smoking is inevitable.

I believe that motivation to stop smoking already exists in all smokers. No one can feel happy about doing something so antilife and destructive. The problem is not to create motivation, but to uncover it.

Stress. . .

Smokers often believe that smoking helps them cope with stress. This is an illusion.

Certain feelings or situations trigger desires to smoke (withdrawal.) Stress is one of those feelings. So, when you feel stress, there are actually two separate sources of discomfort—the stress and the craving.

If you smoke, one of those sources is eliminated. The craving disappears for a few minutes, and all you are left with is the stress. You do feel better after the cigarette, but not because the stress has lessened. It's because the craving is temporarily gone. If you learn to separate these two distinct phenomena, you will quickly see that smoking doesn't help you cope with stress.

Rationalization. . .

Does smoking make life easier? Or harder?

I used to be convinced that smoking relaxed me, helped me cope with stress, and enabled me to think. Even now, I sometimes think, "Wouldn't a cigarette make things easier?"

Stopping smoking involves moments of difficulty, but overall my life is much easier. I have the same problems I used to, but I cope with them as well or better than I used to. If I smoked now, these problems would not go away—I would just have another huge problem.

Deprivation. . .

Nobody has to stop smoking. Many people have good reasons to. For some smokers it is even a matter of life and death. But no one has to stop smoking. And thinking and acting as though one "has to" is a guaranteed way to make stopping smoking a grim experience.

I am as free to smoke now as I have ever been. I am simply making an intelligent, life–affirming choice, which involves some difficulty at times. Knowing I have this freedom is the difference between feeling good and feeling bad about not smoking.

Pleasure. . .

There is an important difference between pleasure and relief. Smokers feel better after they smoke. But this is not because they get pleasure from smoking—it is because they are less uncomfortable. A desire to smoke is the beginning of withdrawal from the last cigarette. The best smoking can do is take smokers back to the way they would feel if they did not smoke.

But, in fact, most smokers do not even get back to this neutral point—they live with physical discomfort, self–reproach, and an obsession to stop smoking. They feel better after a cigarette, but only because they are superficially less uncomfortable. Smoking is not pleasure—it is just less discomfort in the short run and more discomfort in the long run.

One puff. . .

Your addiction will always lie to you.

The addict inside me whispers, "Let's have just one." Ha! You can't fool me. If I smoke one, you'll just say, "Let's have just one more. And one more. And one more."

If I smoke a cigarette, I will not feel "satisfied." I will just want to smoke more. Even if I smoke one hundred, I will want one more. One cigarette will never "take the edge off" or "calm me down." It will just rekindle my desire to smoke and smoke and smoke.

Anxiety. . .

Anxiety comes from getting off and into the future: "What's going to happen next week? Am I going to blow it on New Year's Eve? Oh my God, I'll never smoke again."

The way to make fear and anxiety disappear is to bring myself back to the present. "I don't know what's going to happen next week. I'll worry about it then. I'll deal with New Year's Eve on New Year's Eve. Maybe I'll smoke again someday, maybe I won't. Right now I'm not smoking, and that's all I need to worry about."

Difficulty. . .

It's perfectly normal for stopping smoking to be difficult.

When I first stopped smoking I really struggled. It was so difficult for me that I became quite demoralized. I thought that I must be doing it "wrong." Then a good friend of mine told me, "Stopping smoking is a messy business. Experiencing difficulty doesn't mean you're doing it wrong—it means you're doing it."

This made a lot of sense to me. Some women have an easy labor, some have a difficult one. It doesn't mean some women do a "better job" than others—it just means our experiences are different. If my stopping smoking is difficult at times, then that's just how it's supposed to be for me.

Cravings. . .

Part of being an adult means accepting life's limitations, and developing realistic goals and expectations.

If I buy a lottery ticket expecting to win, the chances are very high I'm going to be disappointed. And to repeatedly buy tickets with that expectation is to live in misery. On the other hand, if I buy the ticket knowing the odds are a zillion to one against me, I can treat the bet as a game and not be disappointed.

If I expect stopping smoking to be effortless, I will be disappointed when it isn't. If I look at stopping smoking realistically, and know there are going to be ups and downs, I will handle the downs much better, and be happier.

Motivation. . .

"Oughts" and "shoulds" destroy motivation.

There is no rational basis for saying I "should" stop smoking. It's my life and my body, and I can do whatever I want with it. It's true that smoking often creates horrific consequences—but it's my decision whether or not I want to risk them.

I am stopping smoking because I want to, not because I "should" or "have to." If I am clear about this, I feel enthused, motivated, and free.

Maintenance. . .

Most treatment models view recovery as a lifelong process. Addiction is not something you just walk away from. Alcoholics, for instance, often have inpatient treatment and then go to meetings for the rest of their lives. Drug addicts have similar forums. Chemical dependency recovery can not be taken for granted, it must be worked at and maintained for life.

I would be wise to assume the same philosophy about my addiction. I should never take it for granted or think, "I've got it licked." I acknowledge I will need to spend time on it, at least occasionally, for the rest of my life.

Decisions. . .

Making decisions to not smoke is a skill, which needs to be learned and practiced.

During the first few days after I stopped smoking, I spent almost all my time making decisions. I would agonize about how much I wanted to smoke. I would think about the rewards of not smoking. And I would decide for the moment to not smoke. I did this over and over, and making these decisions became steadily easier. Now I do it almost unconsciously. But I don't believe I would be able to make decisions easily now unless I had devoted lots of time to making hard ones in the beginning.

Addiction. . .

Smoking is the most insidious of all addictions.

Alcoholics are lucky. Their addiction makes them so miserable that they have tremendous impetus to stop. A spouse threatening to walk out, a boss about to fire them, physical degeneration, legal problems, all make alcoholics so desperate that they'll often do anything to get sober.

Smokers never experience this. They almost never "hit bottom." The damage smoking does is hidden for such a long time that it's easy to go on smoking.

It requires a greater act of will, more initiative, and a greater struggle for honesty to create the motivation to stop smoking.

Pressure. . .

Praise from others can be a mixed blessing.

A number of my friends have expressed surprise and delight when they have noticed I'm not smoking. On the one hand I like their approval and encouragement. It reaffirms that what I'm doing is worthwhile. On the other hand I feel a little more trapped and pressured, "Boy, I really can't smoke now. Everyone would really be disappointed in me."

The answer to this sense of pressure is the realization that I can, in fact, smoke if I choose to. My friends will get over it. I am not cornered, committed, or trapped in stopping smoking. I'm doing it of my own free will—because I want to.

Insanity. . .

Breaking an addiction can be like saying "no" to a spoiled child.

When I first stopped smoking, my addiction had tantrums. It tried to trick me in incredibly devious ways. It lied, cajoled, manipulated, and pressured. But just like with a real child, I've found that a firm, consistent "no" leads to gradual acceptance. My addiction is learning that "no" means "no."

Honesty. . .

To be dishonest is to be in conflict with reality—a stressful experience. To be honest is to be in harmony with reality, and open to peace and spirituality.

It is very difficult to smoke without dishonesty. To look at yourself in the mirror and really admit that what you are doing is destructive would be too painful. And so smokers always have the added stress that comes from self–deception.

One of the great things about stopping smoking is that I don't have to lie or rationalize it any longer. That was hard work. Honesty feels better, and is far easier.

Vitality. . .

Smoking saps your energy.

As a smoker, I always had a hangover in the morning from my smoking. I woke up groggy, and needed a couple of cups of coffee and a few cigarettes to get myself going. Within a few days of stopping smoking, I started waking up an hour before the alarm would ring. At first I thought there was something wrong because I couldn't go back to sleep. But then I realized I was just refreshed and ready to get up. Now I awake easily, and am ready for action very quickly. I seldom need stimulants like coffee anymore, and I have far more energy than I used to.

Realistic options. . .

Smokers often waste time hoping for magic. They don't want to deal with their addiction—they want it to disappear.

This hope is understandable, but unrealistic. Reality gives me some options, but does not give me others. Just as it is impossible for me to flap my arms and fly, it is impossible for me to become a non–smoker and just forget about smoking. I can however, become an ex–smoker, someone who occasionally gets cravings but chooses not to act on them. If I hope for magic the cravings seem oppressive. If I accept the cravings as a normal part of being an ex–smoker, I can live with them cheerfully.

Addiction. . .

Addiction is a one–way street. You can become an addict, but once you do there is no going back.

For the rest of my life I will be dealing with the consequences of becoming an addicted smoker. I will never be neutral about tobacco. But by acknowledging this fact openly, and dealing with it honestly, I can remain in control of my addiction and feel happy about doing so, one moment at a time.

Confidence. . .

When a goal seems unattainable, we are unlikely to expend energy pursuing it. But when something we want is there for the taking, it's easy to summon up the energy necessary to get it.

Consistent, comfortable abstinence is something I can achieve. It takes work and occasional discomfort, but it is there if I want it. Today I will remember that I can do this.

One puff. . .

If you can see where danger lies, you can avoid it.

Just as alcoholics must always remember they have a problem, and stay on their guard, so must I. Every day I feel more confidence in my ability to stay off smoking. But I must never take that abstinence for granted. I am always one puff away from full–time smoking. I will never be able to smoke "just one" with impunity. And knowing this is the key to success.

One puff and I'm smoking.

Realistic options. . .

Sometimes life gives us choices we do not like: "Get a job or be broke." "Stay in a bad marriage, or go through the wrenching pain of a divorce." "Go on smoking and be miserable, or deal with the difficulty of stopping."

A common source of paralysis is, "I don't want either one of these choices! I'm going to hold out for a third alternative." In stopping smoking, this means hoping against hope for some magic answer that doesn't exist.

Movement and progress only become possible when I accept that it's either smoke or don't smoke.

Gratitude. . .

A good way to cultivate gratitude is to look at other people, and the choices they have made. For instance, there are elderly smokers out there who have damaged their lungs so badly they can barely walk—this makes you think. There are smokers who insist they don't care if they get cancer—will they be singing a different tune someday?

On the other hand there are healthy retirees enjoying the fruit of many hard choices they made over a lifetime—choices to stop smoking, to eat right, to exercise.

Am I laying the groundwork for that kind of happiness?

Paralysis. . .

One factor which can keep people in a rut is an unconscious hope that someone is going to come along and rescue them.

A key turning point in stopping smoking was my admission that, if I didn't take some initiative and make some hard choices, I was going to smoke for the rest of my life. Unless I took responsibility for making this change, it wasn't going to happen. I would ruin my one and only life by smoking.

No one is going to rescue me. If I am going to change, I need to do it.

Cravings. . .

The secret to dealing with cravings is to allow yourself to experience them. If you acknowledge and accept a feeling, you can choose how to deal with it. If you repress or deny a feeling, you often "act it out," in spite of your best efforts at self–control.

In psychology, this is the theoretical basis of neurotic behavior. People who will not or cannot experience certain feelings often act them out—sometimes directly, sometimes symbolically. Much of therapy is directed to bringing out and integrating these repressed feelings.

The more willing I am to experience my cravings, the less likely I am to act them out.

Change. . .

Change is hard. Some people compare it to steering an ocean liner. You turn the wheel and have to hold it very hard, for a long time before the ship begins to turn. Very gradually your course changes, and eventually it becomes easy to stay on the new course.

Stopping smoking is like that. It was difficult at first, but I stuck with it, and now it keeps getting easier.

Party. . .

A game smokers commonly play when trying to stop is: "Maybe I'll just smoke tonight at this party, and tomorrow I'll stop again."

Soon after I stopped smoking, I was tempted to play this game. Then I imagined myself waking up the next morning. My throat was sore. I had a bad taste in my mouth. I felt guilty and depressed. And I wanted to smoke even more.

I didn't smoke at the party. I had a difficult hour or so, watching other smokers and trying to decide what to do. But by the end of the evening I felt great! I felt stronger and better and more committed to stopping smoking than ever.

Moment by moment. . . .

There are no guarantees in life. None of us can really know or decide now what we will do later.

I cannot know what I will do tomorrow, or on New Year's Eve. I can only be in control for this moment. If I do not worry about the future, if I keep myself grounded in the moment, stopping smoking is much easier.

Deprivation. . .

"I can't smoke," is not only untrue, it leaves you in a psychological prison. "I can smoke," is true, and allows you to feel free even if you are choosing not to smoke.

I am as free to smoke now as I have ever been. It's true, it's impossible to smoke **and** be an ex–smoker. It's one or the other. But it's up to me which one I choose. If I am not smoking, it's not because I can't—it's because I choose not to. The difference is crucial.

Denial. . .

Many smokers don't realize how enslaved they are because cigarettes are legal, relatively cheap, and easy to get. In fact, if cigarettes were illegal, many smokers would lie, cheat, and steal to get them. And cigarettes kill more people each year than heroin, cocaine, alcohol, and auto accidents combined.[1]

My abstinence depends in part on my willingness to be honest about the deadly seriousness of this addiction. If I try to minimize it as "just a bad habit," I let my guard down and endanger my abstinence.

---

[1] Approximate number of deaths: Smoking 434,000[2] Heroin and Morphine —2,400[3] Cocaine and Crack—3,300[3] Alcohol (including drunk driving)—105,000[4]

[2] U.S. Centers For Health Statistics, 1988 data

[3] National Center For Health Statistics, 1988 data

[4] U.S. Centers For Disease Control, 1987 data

—as quoted from Smokefree Educational Services, Inc. New York, NY

Humility. . .

Some smokers can stop smoking on their own. Some need a little help. Some need a **lot** of help. The key is to figure out the kind of person you are, and get the appropriate help.

As time goes on I realize that admitting I needed help was one of the crucial steps that enabled me to stop smoking. Lots of people who can't stop smoking refuse to admit it, and go on smoking as a result. Even today I sometimes need to talk to a friend when I'm having a difficult day. I'm not ashamed of needing help—I'm glad I can ask for the help I need.

Procrastination. . .

Fifty million Americans smoke. Probably very few of them are planning to smoke forever. But many of them will. In the meantime, they tell themselves they're going to stop "someday."

"I'll smoke today and quit tomorrow." How many times have I said that to myself? What will be different about tomorrow? "I'll do it tomorrow," will keep me smoking indefinitely, because tomorrow just never comes. It is always today.

Relaxation. . .

What smokers call relaxation is really pseudo–relaxation. Smoking eliminates the discomfort of withdrawal for a very short time. This relief is somewhat more comfortable than withdrawal. But to call it relaxation is false.

Smoking is a tremendous source of physical and psychological tension. The slight lessening of the tension that smokers experience after smoking is not real relaxation.

True relaxation only becomes possible when I stop smoking. Then it is possible for my body to function normally. Then the guilt and self–reproach feel is gone. Then I am open to feelings and inner peace.

Confidence. . .

Stopping smoking is not pain and suffering. It is difficulty, in ever decreasing amounts.

I must not minimize the difficulty of maintaining my control over smoking. At the same time, I must not be melodramatic about it. If I remain true to myself, and use the resources at my disposal, I can deal with my smoking.

Denial. . .

Smoking is a particularly insidious addiction, in part because the damage it does is so hidden.

Today I watched people smoking, seeming so unconcerned, and thought about the day, perhaps many years from now, when they would hear the bad news from the doctor, or start coughing up blood, or just keel over. How will they feel then? They are like people tied to the railroad tracks who say, "No problem. The train is still a ways off." Yes, the train is still a ways off, but for these people, it is definitely coming.

Difficulty. . .

"When life hands you a bowl of lemons, make lemonade!"

Good advice. I take it to mean, make the best of bad situations. My bad situation is that I got myself addicted to cigarettes. And there's no undoing that. But I can make the best of things. I can accept the truth, first of all—that I'll never be a non–smoker. That I'll always have at least some cravings. Second, I can consciously choose the best option I've got—accepting the minor difficulty of not smoking to get the huge rewards it brings. Third, I can really enjoy the pleasure I've earned by not smoking.

One puff. . .

For most smokers, cutting down is not an option.

As a smoker I smoked twenty cigarettes a day. I smoked that many because I couldn't smoke less. I could cut down temporarily, but on a consistent basis, twenty seemed to be my minimum.

I will never be someone who smokes half of what I used to smoke. I will never be someone who smokes just at parties, or just when I'm upset, or just on weekends. As a smoker I have a minimum. If I take one puff of a cigarette, I'm smoking. And I will go right back to my minimum and stay there.

Cutting down, or smoking occasionally, is not an option.

Overconfidence. . .

There is no such thing as "quitting" smoking.

In the past when I stopped smoking, I thought I had quit. I believed that I'd never smoke again and I told people as much. When I returned to smoking, I not only felt bad about my smoking but I also felt foolish because I had told people I had quit.

This time I am approaching my stopping smoking differently. I don't tell myself, or anyone else that I've quit. I now know that when it comes to addiction, there is no such thing as quitting. There is only stopping one moment at a time, and having those moments add up. Now when someone asks me how I'm doing I tell them, "So far—so good."

Cravings. . .

"Happiness is the fruit of the ability and willingness to sacrifice what we want now for what we want eventually."—Steven R. Covey, *7 Habits of Highly Effective People*

I have no reason to be afraid of cravings. I do not have to act on every impulse I get. It is perfectly possible to want to do something, and not do it. In fact, the most satisfying things in life usually require this kind of decision.

Substitutions. . .

It is not uncommon for smokers to gain weight when they stop smoking. This is not so much the result of any "metabolic change," as a sign that they are using food to cover up the difficulty of stopping smoking.

Part of stopping smoking is experiencing and working through cravings and conflict. If I allow myself to have cravings sometimes, and choose to accept these minor discomforts to have a better life, I can quickly learn to live comfortably with those cravings. But if I try to run away from cravings by covering them up with food, I will never really come to terms with them.

I will not cover up my cravings with food. I will allow myself to experience the moderate difficulty of stopping smoking to get the benefits of being an ex–smoker.

Discomfort. . .

All living creatures have an instinct to avoid discomfort. This can range from jerking your hand off of a hot stove, to avoiding thoughts that are unpleasant.

For humans, it is sometimes necessary to override this instinct and deliberately choose to be uncomfortable in order to achieve a greater good. Getting a vaccination, having your teeth worked on, pushing your body in an exercise program are all examples of this. Anyone who avoids all discomfort will have a terrible life.

Today I will deliberately choose to experience the discomfort of cravings, and treat those feelings as a small price to pay for the benefits of not smoking.

Humility. . .

One of the odd aspects of addiction is that a part of your mind turns against you.

I feel at times as though I am locked in a room with a crazy person—one who will say anything, do anything, pull any kind of sneaky trick to get me to smoke. If I realize that it's my addiction talking, and that this voice does not have my best interests at heart, I can see through its seductive tricks and choose not to smoke. In fact, I can even laugh at what a textbook addict I am.

Before I smoke. . .

If someone trying to stop chooses to smoke a cigarette, what are the likely results?

If I light a cigarette, the best case scenario is that I will feel guilty, regretful, and demoralized. And my cravings will come back full force. The worst case scenario is that I will return to smoking.

Before I smoke. . .

Smoking hurts the person doing it more than anyone else.

Yesterday I got furious at my boss. My immediate and strong reaction was, "I'm going downstairs and I'm going to smoke. That will show him."

Then I was amazed at my thinking. It's true that my boss implemented a smoke–free policy at my company a few months ago. It's also true that I chose to stop smoking then. But he didn't, and could never, make me stop smoking. Lighting up would not be rebelling against him—it would simply be a stupid and tragic decision which would hurt only me.

Tolerance. . .

Militant ex–smokers are amazing. When they preach about banning cigarettes, forcing people to stop smoking, restricting smoking even in open air areas, the level of hostility they exhibit is clearly excessive and inappropriate. It's difficult to believe these people are really angry about smoking. They are unhappy people, looking for something to attack, and smokers make a great target.

If a smoker blows smoke in my face, I have a right to object—firmly but respectfully. If I am abusing a smoker, then something else is going on.

Honesty. . .

It is impossible to smoke without feeling the consequences. All smokers have difficulty breathing, impaired circulation, poisons throughout their body, a low energy level, difficulty awakening in the morning, reduced sensory awareness, sore throats, aching chests.

A smoker said to me recently, "I don't feel any health consequences from smoking. I feel fine, and if I didn't I would stop smoking immediately." This person chooses not to be aware of the consequences of smoking.

I believe that this denial is born of despair. People who know what they are doing to themselves, and are afraid they can't stop smoking, deal with that pain and fear by pretending they don't notice or care about the terrible effects of smoking.

Benefits. . .

Smokers often say, "Cigarettes give me a boost."

I used to believe this myself. Now I wonder. I have noticed that marathon runners don't stop at mile fifteen for a nicotine pick–me–up. If anything, the smokers I know seem to have less energy than the non–smokers. And my own experience confirms this observation. I get out of bed much more easily now. Physical exertion seems much less draining. I don't run out of gas in the middle of the afternoon. I'm much more willing to do things and to be involved in life.

Difficulty. . .

Stopping smoking has positives and negatives. The positives are the wonderful physical and psychological benefits that come from not smoking. The negatives are the difficult moments—lots of them early on, fewer as time goes by—that are part of being an ex–smoker.

If I don't accept the negatives, I won't get the benefits. If I'm not willing to pay the price, I don't get the payoff. I will either have both the good and the bad, or I'll have neither because I'll be smoking.

For now, I choose to embrace not smoking—both the difficult moments and the wonderful rewards. I accept it all, good and bad alike.

Freedom. . .

One of the most wonderful benefits of stopping smoking is greater freedom.

My friend's place of business went smoke–free on January 1st. Now he and thirty or forty of his co–workers tramp out to the parking lot to smoke a cigarette twice a day. Rain or shine, 90° above or 20° below, nothing stops them. Every day I walk past this group, and am grateful not to be one of them.

Motivation. . .

Ex–smokers sometimes say: "If I ever get cancer, I'll go back to smoking, because then it won't matter." Underneath this idea is the old addict's fantasy that smoking is a good, pleasant thing to do. And in a situation where the health consequences of smoking did not matter, it would make sense to smoke.

I can't know for sure what I would do if I got cancer, but I hope I wouldn't smoke. I can certainly say now that it would make no sense to smoke. I am very clear that there are plenty of good reasons to not smoke—dignity, serenity, self–esteem—even when health is not a concern.

Rationalization. . .

A common feeling for overeaters or recovering alcoholics who are trying to stop smoking is: "I can't drink. I can't eat. Now I can't even smoke!"

The trap here is the word "can't." If I say this, I am acting as if someone else has forcibly taken away my alcohol, my food, and my cigarettes. I am acting as though I am not responsible for the fact that I am controlling my behavior. And the result is that I experience this control as loss and restriction, rather than gain and growth.

To break out of this negative mind–set, a more responsible approach is needed. "The changes in my life are always up to me. I can drink. I can eat. And I can smoke. If I am not smoking, it's by my own choice."

Confidence. . .

The quickest way to deal with your fear is to face it. The longer you run away from places where you will want to smoke, the longer it will take you to get confident in those situations.

When I thought about stopping smoking, I used to be worried about particular situations, such as card games, or coffee breaks. I wondered how I would get through those times, and wondered if I should avoid difficult situations for a while.

I found that my fear was much worse than anything those situations could bring. I deliberately spent time in all the circumstances where I would want to smoke. I had tough moments, but I got through them. And I developed self–confidence very quickly.

Honesty. . .

It can be hard to trust your own thinking when a large part of the society around you is committed to a lie. "Smoking is good," is an example of this. Fifty million people in the United States smoke, and most of them want to believe they are doing the right thing. Billions of dollars of advertising money spent promoting smoking reinforces this self–deception.

I know smoking is poison— physically, morally, spiritually. If the smokers around me don't want to see that, that's their problem. I will trust my own conclusions.

Excuses. . .

Smokers often blame everything and everyone but themselves for their smoking, "If you had my problems you'd smoke too," or, "I'm under too much stress to stop now." What I eventually learned that turned things around for me is that it's **never** the fault of external circumstances. It's always the decisions I make, and the way I respond to external circumstances. Excuses are baloney.

My abstinence has nothing to do with how smoothly or roughly my life is going. If I smoke, it will not be because I'm under stress, or because I've experienced a tragedy, or because the world isn't the way I want it to be. It will be because I chose to smoke.

Moment by moment. . .

Your problem is never in the future—it's here and now, **only**.

I'm afraid of what's going to happen next weekend. I'm going to be with friends who smoke. Smoking, drinking, and letting everything go have always been such a part of our get–togethers that I don't know how I'm going to make it through without smoking.

Wait a minute. My problem is not next weekend. My only problem is right now, and right now I'm not smoking. I'll worry about next weekend when the time comes. Maybe I'll smoke, and maybe I won't. I have no control over that now. But, here and now I'm OK. All I need to worry about is **this** moment. If I'm not smoking right now, I'm as safe as I can possibly be.

Withdrawal. . .

Smoking is really just trading short–term relief for long–term enslavement.

About 24 hours after I stopped smoking I realized something. These feelings—intense cravings, physical discomfort, deep conflict, and indecision—were the real reasons I smoked. This is what being "hooked" really meant. Each cigarette was simply a decision to postpone withdrawal for another few hours. The justifications for smoking that I had invented so creatively were really just delusions.

Willpower. . .

Many smokers think that if they just had enough willpower they could stop smoking. That's like saying that if you just had enough willpower, you could fly a plane or do nuclear physics.

Stopping smoking is a process you need to learn and practice. It consists of being honest and making decisions responsibly. Some people can work this out for themselves—others need to be shown the way. But, people who can't stop smoking are not necessarily weak—they just don't know how to stop smoking.

Motivation. . .

You create your own motivation.

If I am having a bad day, or feeling poorly motivated, I do not have to passively accept the situation. I can actively take steps to reinforce my motivation. I can remember how I felt as a smoker, and how badly I wanted to stop. I can look for physical and psychological benefits I have gotten from stopping smoking. I can be more honest when I start to rationalize and justify smoking. I can think about how I want my life to be, and how I don't want it to be. I can find a friend to talk to.

A day may start out hard, but there is always something I can do to make it better.

Tolerance. . .

People have a right to smoke if they choose.

It is important that I don't preach or become "holier than thou" with my friends who smoke. By stopping smoking I am making the choice that's right for me. And just as I insist on the right to make my own decisions about my own life, I want to respect the rights of others to do the same. My friends are my friends whether they smoke or not.

Cravings. . .

There is no shame in wanting to smoke sometimes. It's just a fact of life for me, because I made some bad decisions when I was younger and got myself hooked on cigarettes.

I will not judge myself for a natural feeling over which I have no control. Instead I will judge myself by the decisions I make and the actions I take. I will give myself credit for the good decisions I have been making to deal with my smoking.

Benefits. . .

Smoking does not improve concentration—it impairs it.

I think better since I've stopped smoking. Before, if I was craving a cigarette, that would be so distracting that I'd need to smoke before I could pay attention to the matter at hand. I needed to stop and smoke every few minutes so I could go on working.

Now I can just pay attention to what's going on, without the distraction of smoking. My circulation has improved and my brain gets a more normal supply of oxygen, which also helps me think. My ability to concentrate has improved, and therefore my productivity has also improved.

Realistic options. . .

Sometimes life isn't exactly the way you want it. There are times when the best you can do is choose the lesser of two evils. Stopping smoking is like that.

If I had magical powers, I would simply make my addiction disappear, forget about it, and go on with my life. Unfortunately, I don't have magical powers. I only have two less–than–perfect options—to smoke, or live with cravings sometimes. On a good day it's very clear which is the best alternative. If I stop hoping for magic, and look at my real choices, living with cravings doesn't seem too bad.

Loss. . .

There is a difference between wanting something and missing it. When you miss something, the implication is that it's no longer available.

Wanting to smoke is a natural part of being an ex–smoker. But if I miss smoking, I am acting as though I am imprisoned by an irrevocable decision to quit smoking—as though cigarettes are no longer available and I am no longer free to smoke.

When I find my "want" turning into longing or grief, I tell myself, "There's nothing to miss. The cigarettes have not died or been taken away from me. I'm just choosing not to smoke them because I want a better life."

One puff. . .

"When you get run over by a train, it's not the caboose that kills you."—*A.A.* axiom

For an addicted smoker, lighting a cigarette is not just lighting a cigarette. It is almost always **returning to smoking.**

Abstinence is an all or nothing proposition. Smoking a little is like being a little bit pregnant. It's not the hundredth or thousandth cigarette I need to be afraid of—it's the first cigarette.

Denial. . .

Smoking injures anyone who does it. It is impossible to put that poison in your body, year after year, without being hurt. The damage is largely hidden for many years—but it is there just the same.

When I smoked, I used to deal with my fear of cancer and heart attacks by saying things like, "It won't happen to me." I might as well have said, "Actions don't have consequences." It **will** happen to me if I smoke.

Deprivation. . .

Whether you see the glass as half empty or half full depends on your state of mind. In the same way, smoking can be experienced as a profound loss or a wonderful gain. What makes the difference? A responsible attitude. If you act like stopping smoking has been forced on you, like you are a victim being deprived against your will, you will experience stopping smoking as loss or an imprisonment. If you approach stopping smoking as a free choice that you are making for good reasons, you will experience it as rewarding and liberating.

No one is making me do this. I am choosing to do it to have a better life.

Cravings. . .

Sometimes life gives you only two choices—neither one of which is ideal—but one of which is clearly better than the other.

I can never be a nonsmoker. I can live with my desires to smoke, or smoke. But it's one or the other. When I get a craving, that's a sign that I'm not smoking. That I'm picking the best option available to me. Even though cravings can be mildly uncomfortable, I can feel very good about them when I realize they are the only alternative to smoking.

Benefits. . .

Sometimes stopping smoking can produce a déjà vu experience.

I smoked for thirty years. When I stopped, within a few days I could suddenly breathe more easily, and taste and smell the air I was breathing.

This produced a profound emotional experience. The last time I had felt those feelings was as a teenager, before I started smoking. A flood of memories came back to me, like I was suddenly rediscovering a self I had lost sight of. This feeling has persisted and grown, too. I am more whole, more unified, and have access to more of myself now that I have stopped smoking.

Relapse. . .

Thomas Edison needed to try over ten thousand different alloys before he developed a filament for his electric light bulb that worked. After many tries, he said: "I have not failed ten thousand times. I have successfully discovered ten thousand ways that do not work."

What a great attitude! A relapse is not a failure. It is a sign that you have discovered another way that doesn't work, and that it's time to try something new.

Self–Image. . .

You are not your smoking.

Before I stopped smoking, I couldn't imagine myself as an ex–smoker. I had smoked for longer than I remembered, and couldn't imagine any other kind of life. I felt that without the cigarettes, I just wouldn't be me anymore.

I'm really glad now that I took the chance. I'm still here. Cigarettes were not an important part of my identity. I am the same person I was when I smoked—only healthier.

Commitment. . .

Commitment means, in one usage, "to be locked up." It seems like a paradox, but the more you "commit" yourself to not smoking anymore, the more likely it is you will smoke.

A **goal** of staying off smoking is healthy and good. A **commitment** will leave you feeling imprisoned, trapped, and deprived. This trapped feeling makes not smoking unbearable for many people. The best way to maintain a sense of freedom when not smoking is to make your decisions one moment at a time, and deliberately **not** make assumptions or commitments about the future.

I want to stay off smoking. I am capable of staying off smoking. But I'm not "committed." I'm freely choosing to do this for right now.

Freedom. . .

"Smoking is always having to say you're sorry."—Dr. Tom Ferguson, *Dr. Dean Ornish's Program For Reversing Heart Disease*

As a smoker, I always needed to worry when I got close to people. Did I stink? Was my breath horrible? Were they going to make a snide comment, or begin an earnest discussion about my smoking?

I know enough now not to place too much importance on what other people think. I am capable, if need be, of living as a smoker, and not allowing myself to be pushed around by non–smokers. Nevertheless, there is a sense of freedom I have now that I didn't have before. I have less to worry about and I feel more comfortable around people.

Deprivation. . .

Anger, depression, self pity, and anxiety are not really a necessary part of stopping smoking. They come from a mistaken assumption that smokers almost universally make when they are trying to stop; "I can't smoke anymore." This false idea leaves you feeling restricted, angry, and depressed.

In fact, I am free to change my mind and smoke anytime. No one is forcing me to do this. I am not in prison. I am making a free choice, which involves some difficulty, for profound and important rewards. I can smoke—but I am choosing not to for now. Knowing I have this freedom is what defuses the anger, depression, and self–pity.

Motivation. . .

The best motivation is a selfish motivation.

I need to see reasons to stay off smoking that don't involve anyone else. I am the only one who is always here.

If I stop smoking to please my children, what happens if I get furious at them? If my motivation is to get along with my spouse who hates smoking, what will happen if we get divorced?

One of my most important goals is to look for selfish reasons to stay off smoking. Reasons that will matter to me even if no one else ever knows or cares that I've stopped.

One puff. . .

Smokers never want "a cigarette." They want to smoke.

"Let's see: I smoked 30 cigarettes a day for 20 years. 30 x 365 x 20 = 219,000. 219,000 cigarettes? Oh my God! It didn't seem like more than 218,000." Seriously, when you sit down and work these kind of numbers, the results are staggering.

When I look at this calculation, the idea of "just having one" becomes truly laughable. I don't want just one—I want a truckload, a trainload, an avalanche of cigarettes. If I smoke one, I'll just want 218,999 more over the next twenty years.

Fear. . .

Fear, in moderation and as a response to real danger, is healthy and life preserving. Fear in excess is toxic and paralyzing.

Obsessive fear of smoking often arises from an underlying, unspoken assumption, "I am not capable." This assumption can come from past experiences with stopping smoking, or from a general orientation toward life learned in childhood. It can also be reevaluated, and changed. My goal is to recognize any obsessive fear of smoking for what it is: learned, irrational, and inappropriate.

I am capable.

Cravings. . .

If you are not willing to experience unpleasant feelings, you will miss out on many wonderful ones.

Stopping smoking is a good example of this. It means, among other things, that at times I will crave cigarettes, and feel conflict about what is important to me. The only way to avoid these feelings is to continue to smoke. On the other hand, if I allow myself to be uncomfortable at times, and if I spend time thinking through my priorities, I will be able to also experience the happiness and freedom that come from being free of cigarettes. Cravings and conflict are a small price to pay for the benefits of not smoking.

Difficulty. . .

Life is difficult. It is a series of problems to be solved. Contentment and self esteem are not ends in themselves—they are the by-products of facing challenges honestly and courageously.

I can run from the difficulty of my cravings and conflicts, or I can embrace and experience them for a much more satisfying life. Today I will embrace the difficulty of not smoking as a small price to pay for a very worthwhile end.

Gratitude. . .

Gratitude does not just happen—it needs to be worked at.

There are so many pleasures to be had from not smoking. I can taste and smell the air I breathe. I feel clean. I feel good about myself and more comfortable around others. I feel competent and effective, and satisfied at having accomplished something difficult and worthwhile.

Actively looking for these benefits increases my gratitude and satisfaction at stopping smoking.

Humility. . .

Smoking is so much more than just a bad habit. Many experts believe that nicotine is more addictive than heroin. And tobacco kills about 400,000[1] people a year—more than all other drugs combined.

When I reflect on the years I smoked, all the while knowing it could kill me; when I remember the self reproach and guilt I felt; when I think how twisted and dishonest my thinking became—I am in awe of the deep and powerful hold that cigarettes had on me.

[1] Smokefree Educational Services, Inc., New York, NY

Moment by moment. . .

The future is unknowable. In stopping smoking, worrying about what is going to happen later just creates needless anxiety.

It's pointless to worry now about whether or not I will smoke in the future. That is something I can never know. All I have is this moment. If I'm not smoking now, I'm as safe as I can be.

Despair. . .

Sometimes when nothing works, all you can do is hold on.

Today I was nuts! Depressed, tired, wanting to smoke, unable to think straight. All my motivation, everything I'd accomplished, seemed distant and meaningless. I searched my mind for some concept, some principle to hold on to.

After a few hours the cloud just seemed to lift. I didn't think my way out of it, I didn't work my way through it—I just held on until it passed. And when it did I was relieved and happy that I hadn't smoked.

Responsibility. . .

There is no way of knowing whether or not you will choose to smoke at some point.

I am sometimes tempted to deal with this fear by pretending I don't have choices, "I can't go back to smoking," or assuming that the future is predestined, "I will never smoke again." I try to paint myself into a corner because I am afraid of what I will do if I'm free.

The problem is that those self–imposed (and illusory) restrictions are very unpleasant to live with. Like it or not, I am responsible for my actions one moment at a time, and I have no guarantees about the future. If I keep myself grounded in the present, and don't worry about the future, my fear of this uncertainty diminishes.

Motivation. . .

Denial of death is one of the factors which make it easy to go on smoking. Smokers think there will always be time to undo the damage of smoking, "I will stop smoking someday, before the damage gets too serious." This comforting self–deception enables them to go on smoking without feeling too scared.

Life is short. If I face that fact squarely and acknowledge every day, "I'm going to die someday," changes like stopping smoking suddenly seem much more urgent.

I want to get the most out of the short time I have, and that means dealing with my problems **now**.

Choice. . .

Smokers often say things like: "I'm an adult. I enjoy smoking. I have a right to do it if I choose to." Right and wrong. People do have the right to smoke. But is it really such a free choice once they are addicted?

Smoking is not a pleasant addition to life. It is not a behavior smokers can just take or leave. To not smoke for any length of time is to become acutely uncomfortable. The desire to avoid this withdrawal makes smoking a desperate compulsion, not a free choice.

Cravings. . .

"Being hooked" on cigarettes means that anytime you don't smoke for a few hours, you become acutely uncomfortable. A desire to smoke is really just the beginning of withdrawal. By constantly refusing to deal with the short term difficulty of withdrawal, smokers condemn themselves to the long–term misery of smoking. Stopping smoking means reversing the process—trading short term difficulty for long term rewards.

If I have cravings today, I will take them in stride and keep focused on the long term rewards of stopping smoking.

Benefits. . .

You can get used to anything. Smokers often do not realize how far gone their breathing is because the impairment happens so gradually.

Now, even after exercise, I breathe easily and rarely feel short of breath. The wheezing disappeared within a week of stopping smoking. I can taste and smell the air I breathe. I can feel my lungs.

Honesty. . .

There was a TV show recently about a woman who lived with a daily drinker for twenty years, and professed astonishment when informed her husband is an alcoholic.

I shouldn't be surprised at this. I smoked for years and chose not to be aware of what I was doing. Just as denial enabled the woman on TV to avoid her problem, my own denial kept me smoking for years.

The key is honesty. Only by looking unflinchingly at the truth about our actions can we take steps to change them. This honesty is hard work, and must be practiced continually. Seeing this TV show gave me a renewed respect for the human capacity for self–deception, and a reinvigorated motivation to work toward honesty.

Taking risks. . .

Stopping smoking means taking a risk.

I have stopped smoking many times and I have always gone back to smoking sooner or later. I have no way of knowing I won't fail again this time. But at least I continue to take the risk.

Even if I do smoke someday, at least I tried. I know that there are many smokers who won't even try to stop, because they are afraid of failure. My attempts to stop are reflections of my desire for a better life, my willingness to struggle, and my openness to taking risks.

Even if I do smoke again, I deserve credit for trying.

Decisions. . .

"God grant me the serenity to accept the things I cannot change, the courage to change the things I can, and the wisdom to know the difference."

This profound, helpful prayer can also be restated in purely secular terms. I cannot change that I am an addict, and that I will sometimes have cravings. I can change how I handle those cravings, however, and become an ex–smoker. It involves difficulty at times, but I can do it. And I can be smart enough to stop hoping for magic and deal with my addiction realistically.

Defeatism. . .

People in 12 Step Programs have an expression, "stinking thinking." This means irrational, negative thinking that causes needless despair. Examples include, "Everything's hopeless," "It'll never work," "I'm a failure." This kind of thinking has also been shown to play an important role in many kinds of depression. It has been shown that replacing these thoughts with more rational, balanced, and positive ideas improves mood and makes change more attainable.

When I start thinking, "I know I'm going to fail someday and smoke," I am making a statement I cannot know is true, and which will cause feelings of hopelessness. If I identify that thought as irrational, I will feel better and have more energy and strength for stopping smoking.

Realistic options. . .

Desires to smoke are inevitable, but smoking is not.

As a smoker I chose to smoke when I got cravings. This wasn't inevitable or predestined—it was just the decision I made. I am completely free to respond to these feelings by smoking, or by living with them to get the rewards of not smoking. I am now an ex–smoker because I have been making different choices. Now when I get a craving I just let it sit there until it passes.

Excuses. . .

I spoke to two people who had stopped smoking recently. One had a fight with her boyfriend and smoked. Another lost her husband to a heart attack unexpectedly and continued to **not** smoke.

I take this as evidence that external circumstances are not justifications to begin smoking again. The first woman chose to smoke. If she hadn't had that fight with her boyfriend, she would have found another excuse. Talking to her later, I know she deeply regretted smoking. The second woman dealt with her tragedy, and later told me that through her grieving she was able to feel good that at least she wasn't smoking!

When I smoke, it's **never** the fault of circumstances, it's never inevitable. It's a decision I make.

Cravings. . .

An ex–smoker, by definition, lives with desires to smoke sometimes. Control and abstinence come from accepting these desires **unconditionally**.

If I try to accept these feelings conditionally, I will probably smoke. In other words, if I say, "I will accept the minor stress of not smoking unless there are cigarettes around," or, "Unless I'm under stress," or, "Unless I'm feeling depressed," I am likely to smoke when I get into these situations. But, if I am willing to experience these feelings anytime they arise, I will always have control.

Habit. . .

Sometimes a smoker will say, "I don't stop smoking because it's just a habit." Think about the philosophy underlying this idea. I've been smoking for a long time, it's a habit. Therefore I should continue to do it.

In other words, find a rut, furnish it, and move in. Never question or reevaluate. Never change or grow. If you've been doing things a certain way, just keep doing it that way.

As a smoker, I had a habit that was killing me. A habit I'm much better off without.

Motivation. . .

One reason smokers have poor motivation to stop smoking is that they have spent years creating delusional systems to justify their smoking. Examples of these delusions include: "I enjoy it," "It helps me deal with stress," "It helps me concentrate," "It relaxes me."

These are nothing but the typical rationalizations of an addict. Alcoholics, heroin addicts, and overeaters say exactly the same things.

The real reason I smoke is because I don't want to experience the cravings I have created by becoming an addict. Scraping away the delusions—and admitting that the real reason I smoke is just my desire for an addictive "fix" immediately improves my motivation to stop.

One puff. . .

One cigarette will never be enough. Ten thousand will never be enough. No matter how many a smoker smokes, he or she always wants more.

"All I want is one." If I am honest, I know this is not true. If I smoke one I'll say "just one more." And then I'll smoke another. And another. And I'm off and running.

Cravings. . .

For an ex–smoker, it is normal and inevitable to want to smoke sometimes. The secret to dealing with that feeling is to accept it.

In the past, when I have attempted to stop smoking, I did everything I could to avoid wanting to smoke—eating more, staying busy, chewing gum, exercising more and staying away from situations where I knew I would want to smoke. The more I tried to push the desire to smoke out of my mind, the more obsessed I became.

If I fight the desire to smoke, I get tense and frustrated. If I treat the craving as a normal part of life, and let it come and go, I can live with it.

Fantasy. . .

Ex–smokers sometimes create a fantasy about what smoking again would be like. "It would be so great to sit on my boat, feel the breeze, watch the sunset, and smoke a cigarette."

The problem is that when you actually smoke—it ain't so beautiful. Shortly after lighting up, the fantasy evaporates, and you are left with a bad taste in your mouth, a feeling of fear and self–reproach, deep regret that you smoked.

I can sit in a boat and smoke if I want to. But would it really be so great? How would I really feel? And would it end there?

Benefits. . .

Smoking is antilife.

It's amazing how stopping smoking has increased my stamina. Just going up a flight of stairs used to take the wind out of me. Walking a few blocks was a noticeable strain. I ran out of gas quickly when I played Frisbee with my kids. My life was limited in ways I didn't even realize.

Now my body does more and needs less time to recover than before. This is one of the most beautiful benefits I have gotten from stopping smoking. What it means in sum is that life is easier now, and more possibilities are open to me.

Rebellion . . .

Some smokers maintain that they smoke out of rebellion. They do not like being told what to do. They do not want to be another sheep following the herd.

Independence is not stubbornly doing the opposite of what others are encouraging, whether it's good or bad for me. If it were, jumping off a bridge when others tell me not to would be a sign of independence. Real independence is being able to listen to other people's suggestions and ideas, and then make my own decisions. If I can keep other peoples opinions in perspective, and truly think independently about the pros and cons of stopping smoking, the image of smoking as rebellion and freedom will seem transparently false.

Deprivation. . .

"I can't smoke and be healthy."

True, but this doesn't mean I can't smoke. It means smoking and good health are mutually exclusive. I can have smoking or good health, but it's impossible to have both.

This statement can be dangerous if I misinterpret it to mean, "I can't smoke." It doesn't mean that at all. It just means that if I do smoke I will not be healthy. I still have the option to smoke and take the consequences. If I am clear about this, I will experience stopping as a free choice made for good reasons, not a restriction or obligation.

Pleasure. . .

"There's more to life than sex—there's smoking in the dark afterwards."—Woody Allen, *Without Feathers*

A cute saying, but the facts are that few things hurt your sex life like smoking. Smoking numbs you and robs you of sensitivity. It saps your energy and makes you smell bad. It lowers men's sperm count and sexual performance.

Stopping smoking can only improve my sex life. I have more energy. I feel cleaner and more alive. I am more sensual. I am more open in every way, and more relaxed lying in the dark afterwards.

Feelings. . .

Smoking is a way of not feeling.

To stop smoking is to open myself to feelings—good and bad. A barrier is removed between myself and others—a mixed blessing. It makes it possible to feel at peace with myself, and with the larger reality I am a part of.

Today, instead of focusing on "not smoking" (a non–action), I will instead strive to feel my feelings without judgments, and to be open to what is going on around me.

Crutch. . .

Is smoking a crutch—or a burden?

I used to say, "Smoking helps me cope. It's my crutch." But is it really? Does smoking make life easier or harder?

Although I do crave cigarettes sometimes, I cannot think of a single way in which smoking would make life easier. On the contrary, it would cost money, take time, and cause me to stink and feel bad about myself. It is normal to want to smoke sometimes. But the delusion that smoking helps me cope is false and dangerous.

It gets easier. . .

It really does get easier.

My first few days of not smoking were very difficult. I was thinking about smoking constantly. I was physically uncomfortable. I was in deep, deep conflict. My mind was throwing every game it could at me to get me to smoke. It was an intense struggle.

Now, I get cravings much less often. They last a moment or two, and then pass. The conflict has also diminished—I hardly need to think about whether or not to smoke. Not only is the physical discomfort gone, but my body actually feels great. It has gotten much easier, and will continue to in the future.

Difficulty. . .

Stopping smoking involves ups and downs.

Last night was my toughest time in weeks. It was the annual company party, which I have always enjoyed, and where a lot of people do a lot of heavy smoking. Not only was I obsessed with smoking, I was angry and disappointed that I was having a hard time. Why isn't this behind me? Why isn't it easier?

Stopping smoking is hard sometimes. But if I take a step back and look at the big picture, I have to admit it's gotten much easier. And in spite of difficult moments, it will keep getting easier.

Hope. . .

Sometimes the only thing to hold on to is the idea that, "This too shall pass."

When I have a bad day, I sometimes simply can not think my way through the difficulty I'm having. All I can do is hang on.

Stopping smoking, like everything else, has it's ups and downs. If I think for a moment, I can remember other days where all I wanted to do was smoke. Where nothing else seemed to matter. Where my mind just wouldn't work right. Those days have gotten less frequent since I've stopped smoking.

Stress. . .

Smokers, like many addicts, have a kind of tunnel vision that causes everything to look distorted. For instance, take the idea: smoking helps me deal with stress.

This is true in a very limited sense. A cigarette does relieve the stress of wanting to smoke—for a short time. But overall smoking causes much more stress than the individual cigarette relieves. This is analogous to what happens with an alcoholic—a drink may make him feel better, but drinking ruins his life.

Being an addict. . .

"Addicted" does not mean weak or morally depraved. It means you made a bad decision years ago—a decision to which you may have been genetically predisposed. It is in no way a reflection of your strength, honesty, or character. And it's a mistake to judge yourself for something over which you have no control.

"I'm an addict" is no cause for shame. It is a simple act of honesty, and enables me to move forward in my abstinence and my life.

Delusions. . .

Smokers will sometimes say, "Cigarettes are my friends. They're the only thing I can always count on to be there."

Since I've stopped smoking I've gradually come to reevaluate this idea. First, I can easily imagine an alcoholic saying the exact same thing about his daily fifth of booze. Sometimes we can be very mistaken as to who our friends are.

Second, the cigarettes are still here. I am as free to smoke them as I ever was. They are as available as they ever were—the question is whether or not they are really my friend.

Addiction. . .

Why is it some people get addicted to things right and left and others do not?

Science tells us there is an "addictive personality." Recent research indicates there may be a strong genetic component to this phenomenon. For instance, studies of identical twins separated at birth show if one twin smokes, there is a higher–than–normal probability that the other one will, too.

The "why" is interesting, but ultimately not that important. For whatever reason, I am a tobacco addict, and need to deal with that.

Cravings. . .

Part of maturity—and happiness—is accepting reality. To the extent that you are in conflict with reality, you will be tense and unhappy. With acceptance you will find peace.

Part of finding peace as an ex–smoker is accepting the desire to smoke. These feelings are a normal and inevitable part of being an addict. If I try to avoid them I will feel tense and frustrated. If I expect them, and accept them, I can be comfortable with them.

Relapse. . .

It is human to make mistakes. It is wise to learn from them.

Soon after I stopped smoking, I "slipped" and smoked one cigarette. I felt like a failure—ashamed and scared.

A "slip" is not the end of the world. First of all, I know from past experience that beating myself up over this won't help. I made a poor choice, but I am not a failure. And I am not doomed to go back to smoking if I figure out what problems led me to smoke and work through them.

Benefits. . .

Smokers invest a lot of time and energy in rationalizing. This is because they feel guilty about smoking. So they concoct elaborate justifications to assuage the guilt.

How wonderful not to need to do that anymore! When I cut through all the garbage, smoking was simply not OK with me. Going through complicated mental gymnastics to justify it was exhausting. It feels much better to not smoke.

Cravings. . .

Being an ex–smoker means accepting, and even embracing the desire to smoke. The desire is the only alternative to smoking.

If I ever smoke again, it will not be because I really wanted to smoke. It will be because I wasn't willing to experience that feeling. Lighting a cigarette is really just a refusal to deal with the desire to smoke. The more I can see wanting to smoke in positive terms, the less likely I am to smoke.

Deprivation. . .

When an ex–smoker makes assumptions about the future, that future usually looks pretty bleak.

This morning I woke up feeling like I didn't even want to get out of bed. A whole day ahead of me without smoking! Then I realized I had gotten ahead of myself. Of course my goal was to get through the day without smoking. But could I really know ahead of time whether or not I would do that? When I make assumptions about the future, the future looks bleak. When I stay in the moment, I can feel positive about the moment, and hopeful about the future.

Denial. . .

Smokers practice selective awareness. There are many aspects of smoking they simply choose not to think about. This psychological defense enables them to go on smoking without feeling too terrible about it.

For example, now that I've stopped smoking, I'm acutely aware of the odor emanating from smokers. It's strong, unpleasant, and immediately recognizable. I used to smell like this too, but chose not to be aware of it.

Now that I've stopped smoking, I'm freer to think about this as a general issue in my life. What else do I choose not to see? Stopping smoking is not an isolated issue. It is related to how I deal with life, and intimately connected with my growth as a person.

Fear. . . .

Life is uncertain. The future is inherently unknowable.

I cannot know whether I will smoke again or not. What I can know is that here and now I am not smoking, and that I am capable of making the same decision one moment at a time. For now, I will take pleasure in the moment, and accept the uncertainty of the future.

Forgiveness. . .

To err is human.

On occasion I get a flash of anger, "What a jerk I was to ever start smoking." Well, maybe I was. People are capable of making mistakes, and in this particular, mistake I have about fifty million people for company. Instead of beating myself up for something I did many years ago, I'm going to give myself credit for not smoking now.

Pressure. . .

When a smoker makes a grand announcement that he or she is stopping smoking, that announcement can cause big problems. First, the more a smoker is being watched by those around him, the more trapped and pressured he or she will feel.

Second, motivation becomes confused, "Am I stopping smoking for myself, or for the approval of other people?

For now, I will not discuss this, except with my closest friends or under special circumstances. And when I do choose to talk about it, I will do so in a way that keeps me free from pressure, "I'm working on it. We'll see how it goes."

Motivation. . .

A "victim" mind–set undermines motivation. "I can't smoke" makes it impossible to evaluate the pros and cons of smoking versus not smoking. Smoking simply becomes the forbidden fruit—romantic, attractive, unattainable.

A more responsible attitude, such as, "I can smoke. I'm stopping of my own free will, and I can change my mind if I want to," makes real motivation possible. If I acknowledge that I have choices, I am free to evaluate those choices.

It is only the conviction that I am free to smoke or not smoke that enables me to weigh these two options, and form an opinion about which is more important.

Difficulty. . .

There are many ways to deal with difficulty. One is to evade it. Most of the rationalizations and self–deception practiced by smokers have one purpose only: to evade the difficulty of stopping smoking. Ironically, people who do this ultimately get much more difficulty than they avoid. Another way to deal with difficulty is to face it head on, honestly and responsibly. People who do this—and stopping smoking is a good example of this—actually end up with much easier lives as a result. And they get the deep, almost spiritual satisfaction that comes from facing and overcoming a hard challenge.

Today I'm glad I'm not taking the "easy way out" by smoking. In the long run smoking is much harder, and much less satisfying than facing my problem.

Decisions. . .

Stopping smoking means making deliberate decisions to embrace difficulty sometimes. If you are not willing to live with the cravings, you will not get the benefits of not smoking.

If a craving comes, I will embrace it. Not because it feels good, but because it's the only alternative to smoking. I'll allow myself to experience it because it means I'm not smoking, and that I'm getting the benefits of being an ex–smoker.

Benefits. . .

The "lift" smokers claim to get from cigarettes is an illusion.

I have noticed a paradox lately: I am at once more relaxed **and** more energized than when I smoked. Chain smoking and drinking coffee used to whip me up into a frenzy—and I could get things done in this state for short bursts. But then I would come down with a crash.

Now I experience a quiet, relaxed energy. I can make a sustained effort for a longer period of time, and not be exhausted afterwards. And the bottom line is that I feel better and am more productive.

Delusions. . .

When your mind doesn't work, don't use it.

Usually when I'm having a hard day I can think my way into a better place. But some days I can't. Some days I feel like nothing matters except smoking. Like stopping smoking is pointless. Like the rewards of stopping are meaningless. Like I don't have the strength to go on.

The best thing I can do on days like that is stop listening to my mind. "Today I'm not able to think straight. I shouldn't trust anything my mind is telling me. I know that tomorrow stopping smoking will seem important and rewarding again."

Collusion. . .

Just as addicts deceive themselves with rationalizations and justifications for behavior they really know is wrong, addicts conspire to reinforce each others' excuses. Put two addicts in a room together, and they will often talk each other into using. Most smokers have friends they smoke with, people who "agree" with and reinforce dishonest justifications for smoking. When one person in a group like this stops smoking, the others will even sometimes try to undermine them, so that they won't need to look at their own behavior.

In attempting to become more honest about my smoking, I need to think about ways in which my friends and I helped each other to be dishonest, and be on the lookout for that behavior now.

Higher Power. . .

Whether you believe in God or not, all of us need help from outside ourselves sometimes.

I like the Alcoholics Anonymous concept of a "Higher Power," which can be understood in religious or secular terms. No man is an island. All of us need help and support. Stopping smoking is very difficult, and a crucial part of recovery is asking for help, and looking for strength wherever it can be found. This can mean prayer, Smokers Anonymous meetings, inspirational reading, or contact with friends.

This is not weakness—it is just being human.

One puff. . .

For most smokers, there is no such thing as controlled smoking.

I have friends in Alcoholics Anonymous. I hear a fair amount about this impressive program, and relate it to my own struggle with addiction.

For instance, one of the most common stumbling blocks on the road to sobriety seems to be an inability to admit "powerlessness." In other words, people flirt with sobriety, and then, against all the evidence, decide to try to drink in a controlled way. My friends call this "doing research and development." Because these people invariably test and prove a point—that when they drink they go completely out of control—I'm sure if I lit a cigarette, I'd prove the same point.

Honesty. . .

One way that people handle pain is to repress it.

I have a friend whose life is going nowhere. He can't find a career he likes, or one that brings in money. He tells people that he's not materialistic, and I know that deep down he feels very badly about himself. He's stuck, and the only way he can deal with his anguish is to tell himself he doesn't care.

Many smokers do the same thing. The way they handle their fear and hopelessness is to tell themselves things like, "I don't care if I get cancer," or even, "I don't believe smoking causes cancer." Tragically, it is this denial which prevents growth and change.

The first step toward changing a situation is letting yourself acknowledge how badly you feel about it.

Motivation. . .

Life can be a series of triumphs or a series of failures. I suppose that for human beings it is always a mixture, but I want this to be one of my triumphs. I remember how demoralized and guilt ridden I have felt after returning to smoking in the past. And I'm struck by how often I have taken pleasure, this time, in my continued abstinence.

I want this satisfaction to continue. I want to use this triumph as a stepping–stone to other triumphs. I want my life to continue to grow and get better. I want to continue to be an ex–smoker.

Fear. . .

Fear, in moderation, is essential to survival. It is healthy fear that causes drivers to take their task seriously and be cautious. It is healthy fear that causes people to look both ways before they cross the street. It is a reasonable and sane fear that motivates people to stop smoking.

My healthy fear of returning to smoking is one of my most useful allies. It keeps me on my toes, and motivates me to do what is necessary to maintain my abstinence.

Tolerance. . .

It is useless to try and push people to stop smoking. Suggest it, they give you a rationalization. Deal with the rationalization, they give you another. Keep pushing, they react like a cornered animal.

All I can do is control my own smoking. By doing that, I will set an example that will have an effect on the people around me. But that is the limit of my ability to change others. I will wish other people well, but not try to change them.

Before I smoke. . .

There is never a good reason to smoke. There are only excuses.

If I smoke, I have no one to blame but myself. I chose to do it, but I didn't have to do it. It's not the fault of stress or circumstances—those are just the excuses I use. And as long as I look for excuses I will find them.

Energy. . .

Smokers have less energy than ex–smokers.

One of the rationalizations I used to feed myself about smoking was that smoking energized me. However, the "buzz" I got from smoking wasn't a real energy boost. Like the lift people get from most artificial stimulants, this buzz is short term, and is immediately followed by a let–down. Overall smokers have less energy than those who don't smoke. I knew this deep down as a smoker, and I have more energy since I stopped.

Cravings. . .

For smokers, a desire to smoke is just the beginning of withdrawal. Each cigarette is a decision to avoid the withdrawal from the last cigarette. And then the withdrawal comes right back. Two–pack–a–day smokers, for instance, go in and out of withdrawal forty times a day. By refusing to deal with the short term difficulty of withdrawal, they ensure the withdrawal will return again and again.

As an ex–smoker, I have been out of withdrawal since a few days after I stopped. I have the occasional craving, but as long as I accept it I will never need to deal with withdrawal again.

Deprivation. . .

Knowing that stopping smoking is a free choice—not an obligation—is the key to feeling good about it.

Am I doing this because I have to? Or, because I want to? The difference is crucial. When I take the position that, "I have to," I start to feel trapped, pressured, and deprived.

I am as free to smoke now as I have ever been. I am simply making an intelligent, life affirming choice, which involves some difficulty at times. Knowing I have this freedom is the difference between feeling good and feeling bad about not smoking.

Avoidance. . .

Stopping smoking successfully means learning to live with the desire to smoke, not avoiding it. By living life normally, and facing the cravings in the situations in which they normally arise, you can learn to live with this feeling and not be intimidated by it. Facing a problem is usually easier than running away from it.

In the past, when I tried to stop smoking, I always tried to avoid the situations where I smoked. I was running away from my cravings. There always came a time when I could no longer avoid that feeling. At that point I always smoked. Now I treat the craving as a normal feeling that can't make me do anything. I don't try to avoid it. I live my life, and take the cravings in stride.

Peace of mind. . .

One of the most important rewards of stopping smoking is peace of mind.

Now that I've stopped smoking, I have much less to worry about. When I smoked, sometimes my heart would pound so hard I'd be afraid it was going to burst out of my chest. I would worry about cancer and emphysema, and whether or not I left a cigarette burning when I left home. When I was near people I was afraid that I smelled horrible, or had smoker's breath.

I live with much less fear now. My chances of emphysema are only one tenth of what they were. When I've been off cigarettes two years, my risk of heart disease will have returned to that of the general population. My life expectancy has gone up, and will continue to rise.

Pressure from others. . .

You can not always count on other people.

A friend of mine just called me in tears after a talk with her boss. "He is an ex–smoker so I thought he would understand when I told him I was stopping smoking and it had been 24 hours since I had had a cigarette. Instead of congratulations, he told me I'd probably be smoking in a month. How could he say such a thing?"

In truth, that was a lousy thing for her supervisor to say. Who knows what his problem is? As in every aspect of life, you are going to get healthy responses from some people, and unhealthy responses from others. I suggested that she drop her supervisor from her list of confidants and look for support from people who she knew would be supportive.

Denial. . .

Over 400,000 people die each year in the U.S. from tobacco related illnesses. That is more Americans than were killed in World War I, Korea, and Vietnam put together. [1]

Every year! If a new disease appeared which killed this many people, a national emergency would be declared. But the lethality of cigarettes is calmly accepted, largely for the following reasons:

Smoking has a social acceptability no other addiction can claim.

The damage smoking does takes so long to show up, it's easy to ignore.

Cigarettes are cheap and legal.

Cigarettes are the most heavily advertised product in the world.

In spite of society's complacency, cigarettes kill. I must not forget that this is life and death.

[1] *Acts of War*, Richard Holmes, Free Press, 1985

Withdrawal. . .

Much of the physical discomfort of withdrawal is caused by healthy, healing changes taking place inside your body. These feelings seem unpleasant at first, but begin to feel good as your body adjusts.

For instance, within 24 hours of stopping smoking, most people experience a sudden improvement in circulation. This causes a "spacy" feeling because the brain is getting more oxygen than it is used to. Some get a "pins and needles" sensation under the skin, because the nerve endings there are getting more blood. Light and sound often seem magnified, simply because one can see and hear better suddenly.

Putting the symptoms of withdrawal into a positive context makes them much easier to deal with.

Feeling good. . .

It is not enough to know you are an addict. You also need to find a way not to smoke and feel good about it.

Feeling good when not smoking involves several factors. First, a clear sense of freedom, "I'm doing this because I want to, not because I have to."

Second, a realistic time frame, "I'm not smoking for right now."

Third, an acceptance of the real options, "I can be a smoker or an ex–smoker, I'll never be a non–smoker."

Lastly, a clear sense of the dangers I'll avoid and the benefits I'll get by choosing to live with my cravings.

Cravings. . .

Smokers can be endlessly creative in dreaming up reasons to smoke: "It would relax me." "It would relieve the boredom." "I would be able to enjoy this situation so much more." "It would kill the germs in my throat so I wouldn't get colds."

Underneath all this nonsense, I'm just an addict who wants my fix. I try to dress it up, to put a nice face on it, but underneath I'm just an addict who wants my fix.

Habit. . .

Anything you do thousands of times will become habitual. Smoking certainly becomes a part of a smoker's daily life, and smokers routinely light cigarettes without giving it much thought. But to say that smoking is **only** a habit is to seriously underestimate it; and the evidence is the difficulty smokers have in stopping.

Habits do not enslave people the way smoking enslaved me. I resolved to stop dozens of times and did not do so. I had a genuine fear of the positively lethal effects of smoking, but continued to do it anyway. I felt tremendous anguish and self-reproach over my smoking, but didn't stop. These are not the characteristics of a habit. These are the characteristics of an addiction.

Privacy. . .

The best motivation is personal motivation.

I have found that I feel better if I keep my stopping smoking a private matter from everyone except my closest friends. Several times when socializing I have volunteered that I haven't been smoking. The people I was with were pleased and I felt momentarily gratified, then some-how let down. Their approval doesn't go very far.

The real person I need to please is me. I know I'm doing the right thing, and I feel good about it. The less I look for or worry about other people's approval, the better.

Responsibility. . .

Occasionally smokers will say something to their friends and family like, "I'm trying to stop smoking. I'm probably going to be very irritable for a week or so. I want you to know that if I say anything hurtful, it's not you—it's just that I'm going through withdrawal."

It would be far more responsible, in my opinion, to take the blame for what you are going through, and not abuse others at all. Irritability when stopping smoking is mostly just blaming others, and that doesn't help you or them. "It's my problem, not theirs. They're not doing anything to me. If I don't want to stop smoking, I don't have to."

Deprivation. . .

"If I want good health I can't smoke."

First of all, this is not true. All smokers want good health. They smoke anyway. A desire for good health is just a goal—you are free to pursue it or not.

Second, this kind of confused thinking poisons the experience of stopping smoking. When you tell yourself, "I can't smoke," you are acting like a victim, as if you have no choice about what you are doing. As a result of this thinking you will tend to feel trapped, restricted, and depressed when you are not smoking.

I want good health—but it's my choice. I'm stopping because I want to, not because I have to.

Moment by moment. . .

The future is inherently unknowable. We live our lives in the
present, and hope for the best.

If I acknowledge the simple
fact that I cannot know if I will ever
smoke again, I am not being negative or pessimistic. It doesn't mean
I don't care deeply about staying
off smoking. It doesn't mean the
odds are 90% that I'll smoke, or
10%. It just means I can't predict
the future. I'm living my life one
moment at a time, and not worrying
about the future.

One puff. . .

What would you think if you heard an alcoholic say: "I'm just going to have one drink?" Crazy, right? Yet smokers tell themselves this "just one" lie surprisingly often.

I know I will never smoke "just one" cigarette. If I light up I'm out of control. This knowledge is extremely helpful. I may light up someday—no one can predict the future. But at least I won't smoke thinking it will be just one cigarette. I will know exactly what I'm getting into. That knowledge helps me think twice before smoking.

Happiness. . .

Stopping smoking is **not** about being a virtuous person or living forever. It **is** about feeling happier here and now.

The real point of stopping smoking is that it lets me be happier. Yes, I care about the fact that I will live longer. I care about being healthier, and reducing my chance of disease. But the immediate reason I'm doing this is because, on most days, I just feel happier not smoking.

Risk. . .

Stopping smoking involves risks—and opportunities.

I recently heard someone say, "I don't want to try to stop smoking because I'm afraid I might fail." Think about that as a philosophy of life! There is no possibility of growth without risk. People who don't take chances have terrible lives. They don't grow, they don't achieve, they can't have any self–esteem. The old saying is true, "Nothing ventured, nothing gained."

Self–Love. . .

Stopping smoking is an act of self–love. It represents my willingness to struggle, to create the very best life for myself that I can.

Stopping will enhance my life in every way imaginable. It will give me more confidence in myself and in my ability to solve life's problems. My self–esteem will rise, and I will be far more ready to take on and succeed at other challenges. I will be moving forward, not standing still.

Benefits. . .

One of the most important benefits of stopping smoking is the improvement in circulation that results. The brain gets more oxygen, which helps the thinking process. The optic and auditory nerves become more sensitive, improving sight and hearing. The blood flow to skin increases, which reduces wrinkling and improves the complexion. The nerve endings under the skin work better, which improves the sense of touch, and enables a person to enjoy sensual experiences. Hands and feet are warmer, because blood flow is increased.

I will try to be aware of the improved input provided by my senses, and enjoy the added sensitivity I have gotten from stopping smoking.

Responsibility. . .

We are all free to do whatever we want with our lives.

My life is my own creation. It is a script I can write any way I want to. If I decide to stop smoking, I can do that. If I decide to smoke, I can do that. But whatever happens will be my own responsibility and my own fault. I am not doomed, nor is any particular outcome guaranteed. I am the source and cause of my actions. External situations and events are irrelevant.

This freedom is both scary and exhilarating. Scary because there is no guarantee I won't make bad choices. Exhilarating because there are no limits—I can create any life I want to.

Rationalization. . .

Smokers sometimes use the rationalization: "The damage is already done. It won't make any difference if I stop."

This is patently false. No matter how little or how much damage you have done to your body, it begins to repair itself almost immediately when you stop smoking. Even if you already have cancer, emphysema, or heart disease, your health will improve and your life expectancy will go up if you stop.

I will not tell myself it makes no difference whether I smoke or not. It makes a **big** difference.

Relaxation. . .

One of the most common reasons smokers give for smoking is: "It relaxes me." In fact, this relaxation is largely illusory.

Smoking creates tension physically and psychologically. Each cigarette relieves only a small part of that extra tension. In other words, you do feel more relaxed after a cigarette, but not nearly as relaxed as you would feel if you didn't smoke.

Consciousness. . .

The philosopher Ayn Rand said, "Man is a creature of volitional consciousness."[1]

In other words, while the functions of our heart and stomach are automatic, the functions of our conscious mind are not. We can choose to think and be aware, or to not think and be unconscious.

Smokers practice unconsciousness. They try not to think about or see what they are doing. It is this choice to not think honestly that enables them to continue smoking.

Stopping smoking involves deliberate choices to see, think, and be aware. As such, stopping smoking is not an isolated issue—it is intimately related to my general growth and happiness as a person.

[1] *An Introduction To Objectivist Epistomology*

Enslavement. . .

Price is no object where addiction is concerned.

When my father stopped smoking, cigarettes were 35 cents a pack. When I stopped smoking they were $2.00 a pack.

In Europe and Canada, cigarettes are over $5.00 a pack. I saw on the news today that the price of cigarettes in the United States is going up, and that new taxes will make the price go up even further.

I wonder how high they would have needed to raise the price of cigarettes before I would have put my foot down and refused to pay? I don't think there was a limit. If I hadn't decided to stop for other reasons, I probably would have paid anything, just as drug addicts do now.

Awareness. . .

Would I rather smoke or stop smoking?

Today I found inspiration in a strange place—my daughter's storybook, *The Ant and the Grasshopper*. The ant works and plans for the winter. The grasshopper fiddles. When winter comes, the grasshopper starves.

The parallel to smoking is obvious. Smokers are fiddling—and the winter is likely to be brutal. I am working, and if I keep it up, my winter is going to much healthier and happier than theirs.

Relapse. . .

Sometimes relapse is part of the recovery process. A relapse can be treated as an excuse to give up, a learning experience, or as a sign that something needs to change. It is an invitation to go back to the drawing board.

Coping with this addiction in the various situations of life is sometimes a process of trial and error. If one way doesn't work, I'll try another. If I am determined to succeed, I will find a way.

"If at first you don't succeed, try, try again."

Empathy/Forgiveness...

Young people who start smoking are not simply being monumentally stupid. They are coping as best they can with an extremely difficult time in life.

I started smoking as an adolescent—a very painful time in life. I felt self–conscious and awkward, like I didn't belong anywhere. When I smoked, I didn't feel so bad about myself. I felt "cool" for a little while. I could forget my sense of inadequacy and pretend I had it together, at least for a time. Now I realize smoking didn't create self esteem. It didn't really solve any of those painful problems I was facing. What it did was mask the feelings that motivate growth and change. Smoking is a lousy coping mechanism that I don't need anymore.

Index